"If you could somehow blend equal parts
Dietrich Bonhoeffer, Mr. Wizard and the 'Unsinkable' Molly Brown,
you'd get something close to Heather Zempel.
It would be a fascinating experiment,
like those she describes in *Community Is Messy*.
Stories of what worked (and what didn't)
provide countless examples of how
discipleship in community is usually nonlinear,
often random and always messy.
With deep insight and ample humor,
Heather proves that 'mess' is actually a catalyst for spiritual growth."

DAVE TREAT, small groups leader, Asbury UMC, Madison, Alabama,
and chief innovation officer, thinkingsmall.net

# HEATHER ZEMPEL

FOREWORD BY MARK BATTERSON

# COMMUNITY IS MESSY

## THE PERILS AND PROMISE

## OF SMALL GROUP MINISTRY

IVP Books

An imprint of InterVarsity Press
Downers Grove, Illinois

InterVarsity Press
P.O. Box 1400, Downers Grove, IL 60515-1426
World Wide Web: www.ivpress.com
E-mail: email@ivpress.com

InterVarsity Press® is the book-publishing division of InterVarsity Christian Fellowship/USA®,
a movement of students and faculty active on campus at hundreds of universities, colleges and schools
of nursing in the United States of America, and a member movement of the International Fellowship of
Evangelical Students. For information about local and regional activities, write Public Relations
Dept., InterVarsity Christian Fellowship/USA, 6400 Schroeder Rd., P.O. Box 7895, Madison, WI
53707-7895, or visit the IVCF website at <www.intervarsity.org>.

All Scripture quotations, unless otherwise indicated, are taken from the THE HOLY BIBLE, NEW
INTERNATIONAL VERSION®, NIV® Copyright © 1973, 1978, 1984, 2011 by Biblica, Inc.™ Used
by permission. All rights reserved worldwide.

While all stories in this book are true, some names and identifying information in this book have
been changed to protect the privacy of the individuals involved.

Photos on p. 39 taken by Jenna Wall.

Interior design: Beth Hagenberg
Cover design: Cindy Kiple
Images: © Ekely/iStockphoto

ISBN 978-0-8308-3788-5

Printed in the United States of America ∞

Library of Congress Cataloging-in-Publication Data

Zempel, Heather, 1974-
  Community is messy: the perils and promise of small group ministry
/ Heather Zempel.
      p. cm.
  "Praxis."
  Includes bibliographical references.
  ISBN 978-0-8308-3788-5 (pbk.: alk. paper)
  1. Church group work. 2. Small groups—Religious
aspects—Christianity. 3. Communities—Religious
aspects—Christianity. I. Title.
  BV652.2.Z46 2012
  253'.7.—dc23
                                                              20122018658

| P | 18 | 17 | 16 | 15 | 14 | 13 | 12 | 11 | 10 | 9 | 8 | 7 | 6 | 5 | 4 | 3 | 2 | 1 |
|---|----|----|----|----|----|----|----|----|----|---|---|---|---|---|---|---|---|---|
| Y | 27 | 26 | 25 | 24 | 23 | 22 | 21 | 20 | 19 | 18 | 17 | 16 | 15 | 14 | 13 | 12 |

*To Gran Berry,*
*for making messy things beautiful*
*for the past ninety-five years*

# Contents

# Foreword

I've never met anyone more gifted at or passionate about creating authentic community than Heather Zempel. That passion is evident both personally and professionally. Her love for life is absolutely infectious. So is her laugh! And this book is not just an expression of *what she knows*. It's an expression of *who she is*. By the time you're done reading, I think you'll see why Heather is so beloved by National Community Church.

"Community is messy." It sounds so straightforward. And that much is universally understood. *Why* it's messy and *how* messiness actually creates the community and *what* can be done to manage a community's messiness have always proven to be elusive. But Heather has the guts to step into the mess, to dig around in it, and then step back and find the beauty in it. You'll never see community the same way! As you read this book, you'll find something new, something creative, something beautiful.

Heather has given leadership to our discipleship efforts for the past decade. And this I know for sure: we wouldn't be who we are as a church without her! And the task is not an easy one in Washington, D.C., with a demographic that consists primarily of single twenty-somethings. Not only do we deal with political tensions by virtue of our geography, we also have extremely high turnover rates because of the transient nature of the city. Throw in our six multisite locations and you can understand why creating community is complicated and challenging.

Heather has navigated those challenges by creating and recreating community though love and leadership. You'll read how her team has innovated models of discipleship that take into account the uniqueness of each person and the fluidity of any contemporary expression of community. She shares the credit well throughout the book, but without her leadership I suspect the path to whatever success we've had would have been longer and rougher. Heather is an environmental engineer, by training and by instinct, and her unique insights have blessed our community. As you dig into what she's written in *Community Is Messy*, her insights will bless yours as well.

Community is messy. It's also tragic and hilarious and inspiring and frustrating. It's also part of what God has made us for, and part of God's plan for rooting and establishing us in love and bringing us to fullness in Christ. You're going to cringe, laugh, smile and maybe even cry as you read this book, but you're going to come out of it with a renewed confidence that while community is messy, it's also a gift of God.

Enjoy the mess!

*Mark Batterson*
*Lead Pastor, National Community Church*
*Author,* The Circle Maker

# First Things First

## BLOOD, SWEAT AND SPIT

**S**ometimes people talk about community like it's some kinda lovey-dovey, touch-feely part of Christ-centered living. Perhaps it's just me, but I think community is hard. Maybe I'm just a hard person to have community *with*, but my experience points to the difficult truth that community is messy. And discipleship is hard. If we want to experience them, we pay a significant price. A price that could cost us our blood, sweat and spit.

One of my favorite passages of Scripture is found in Paul's second letter to the church in Corinth. Listen to this:

> I have worked much harder, been in prison more frequently, been flogged more severely, and been exposed to death again and again. Five times I received from the Jews the forty lashes minus one. Three times I was beaten with rods, once I was pelted with stones, three times I was shipwrecked, I spent a night and a day in the open sea, I have been constantly on the move.

Here is where Paul starts to sound a bit like Dr. Seuss.

> I have been in danger from rivers, in danger from bandits,
> in danger from my fellow Jews, in danger from Gentiles;
> in danger in the city, in danger in the country, in danger
> at sea; and in danger from false believers. I have labored
> and toiled and have often gone without sleep; I have
> known hunger and thirst and have often gone without
> food; I have been cold and naked. Besides everything else,
> I face daily the pressure of my concern for all the churches.
> (2 Cor 11:23-28)

Paul basically says, "If all of this flogging and shipwrecking and imprisonment and danger weren't enough, I've got you church people to deal with!"

He was committed to the community of God to the point of death. He was bleeding for it.

The sacrament of Communion, which recognizes our union with God and with the community we experience as the people of God, includes the cup—the sign of the new covenant in Christ's blood. Communion is about remembering sacrifice and celebrating the community we have with God through the blood of Christ. Jesus also bled for community.

A Christian prisoner in Cuba was asked to sign a statement containing charges against fellow Christians that would lead to their arrest. He said, "The chain keeps me from signing this."

The officer protested, "But you are not in chains!"

"I am," said the Christian. "I am bound by the chain of witnesses who throughout the centuries gave their lives for Jesus Christ. I am a link in this chain. I will not break it."[1]

Christian community is a bloody thing, as the long list of martyrs from the apostle Paul to those in hostile territory today can attest. Most of us won't *literally* bleed for our faith though.

That's all right, because as much as Christian community is a matter of blood, it's also a matter of sweat. The Gospel writer Mark shows us that faith sometimes shows up in the form of perspiration:

> A few days later, when Jesus again entered Capernaum, the people heard that he had come home. They gathered in such large numbers that there was no room left, not even outside the door, and he preached the word to them. Some men came, bringing to him a paralyzed man, carried by four of them. Since they could not get him to Jesus because of the crowd, they made an opening in the roof above Jesus by digging through it and then lowered the mat the man was lying on. When Jesus saw their faith, he said to the paralyzed man, "Son, your sins are forgiven." (Mk 2:1-5)

Imagine this story with me for just a moment, because I fear we read so quickly we miss the comedy and the adventure. These guys are *insane*. I can only come up with one dignified word to describe them: tenacious. People are heavy, and who knows how far they had to carry this guy. Did any of them consider leaving him behind? If they hadn't insisted on dragging their friend along, they could have gotten to the house early and found a good seat. Instead they carried him to see Jesus and got stuck in standing room only.

When they arrived at the house, they couldn't get in. Now, I would have just resigned myself to reality, recognized that Jesus would stop preaching at some point, and staked out a spot by the stage door to catch him on his way out. That's what rational people do. But people who understand the community of God aren't rational. They embrace the crazy idea that when two or more are gathered, God is truly there, and the supernatural can happen. They dare to believe that a little sweat is the stuff that waters the seeds of miracles.

Sometimes spiritual maturity is measured in the sweat we expel in serving one another and bearing one another's burdens. When we extend our hand to another, we often find God's hand extending as well, to bring healing, restoration and reconciliation.

With holy tenacity, they hauled their friend to the roof—exerting the energy necessary to get themselves to the top and drag him with them. Once there, they dug a hole big enough to lower him.

Stop and imagine that for just a moment. They put a *hole* in a stranger's roof that was large enough for a grown man to fit through. That's the kind of hole that results in significant structural damage and arguably quite a mess. And then there's the issue of exactly how they lowered him. As they constructed a first-century pulley system with their belts and robes, what were the people inside the house thinking? What was Jesus thinking? Scripture gives us an idea: "When Jesus saw their faith, he said to the paralyzed man, 'Son, your sins are forgiven'" (Mk 2:5).

*Their* faith. The paralyzed man found forgiveness and salvation because of the faith of a few friends who demonstrated their faith in the form of sweat. As we keep reading, we see a discussion between Jesus and the Pharisees over the nature of forgiveness, during which Jesus said to the paralyzed man, "'I tell you, get up, take your mat and go home.' He got up, took his mat and walked out in full view of them all. This amazed everyone, and they praised God, saying, 'We have never seen anything like this!'"(Mk 2:11-12).

This is amazing. A paralyzed man on a mat walks away with new faith and new legs because of the commitment his friends made to walk the extra mile, bear his burden and bring him into an environment where he could meet Jesus. That's when the miracle happened.

Who is being transformed because of your faith and the faith of your friends?

There's something about community that draws people into a relationship with Jesus. One man on his own couldn't have brought this man to Jesus. Two men probably couldn't have carried him all the way. It took a community, a brotherhood, a small group.

I'm so thankful for the people who have carried my mat and, in doing so, have introduced me to dimensions of God's heart and character. I think about committed friends like Alan Alvarez—who literally moved my husband and his bed when minor surgery turned out to be more major than we'd hoped and Ryan's aftercare required more than I could carry on my own.

I think about Ruth Walk, who was willing to endure a late-night meal at the Waffle House to talk, to remember and to laugh on the night before Christmas 2000 as my granddaddy lay in hospice care in the last hours of his life.

I think about February 2010, affectionately remembered as Snowmageddon on the East Coast. Ryan and I missed the excitement while visiting his family in Oregon, but then we got stuck. We spent an entire week hopping from city to city, trying to dodge and outrun winter storms to get back home. From Oregon to San Francisco to Denver to Chicago, people like Dave Treat and Amanda Clark opened their homes to us as we lived day-by-day out of our suitcases.

I'm thankful for the people I've met in my small groups who have gone beyond weekly acquaintances to people who have carried my mat both literally and figuratively. People who sweat for me when I couldn't go as far as I needed off the sweat of my own brow. People who sweat to propel me forward in my faith.

Whose sweat propels you forward in your faith?

Community requires us to do stuff that might be viewed as inappropriate in good company. While the idea of bleeding for community might remain a metaphorical necessity for us, the requirement that we sweat for one another isn't.

In addition to the bleeding and the sweating, I would submit that there's another messy moment we see in Scripture that informs the way we're challenged to relate to others as we strive to follow Christ. Jesus was willing to get down into the mess of life. He touched lepers, befriended despised people and hung out with notorious sinners. A few years ago, it struck me that many of Jesus' miracles of healing were as much about social reconciliation as they were about physical restoration. For instance, after he healed the lepers, he sent them back to the priest. Why? Because the priest was the only person with the authority to pronounce them clean and restore them to society. Jesus healed the outcasts so they could have relationship again.

One of my favorite stories about Jesus entering into the mess is in John 9. Jesus and the disciples encountered a man who was born blind, so the disciples began to question why he was in that predicament—because of his sins or the sins of his family? Fingers were pointed. Assumptions were made. (We often try to avoid messes by spiritualizing them.) Jesus responded by checking the "none of the above" box and claiming the man was born blind to display the glory of God. And this is what happened next:

> After saying this, he spit on the ground, made some mud with the saliva, and put it on the man's eyes. "Go," he told him, "wash in the Pool of Siloam" (this word means Sent). So the man went and washed, and came home seeing. (Jn 9:6-7)

This story is packed with amazing theological depth and richness. We could talk about why Jesus chose to heal in this particular way, or we could ponder the myriad and quirky ways in which God chooses to display his glory. We could explore the first-century Jewish understanding of sin and its physical repercussions or pontificate on the connection between healing and praise.

But I'm not that deep. Here's the question that perplexes me: How many times did Jesus have to spit in that dry, dusty, first-century Palestinian dirt to make that mud?

Jesus Christ, the son of God, spitting and spitting into the dry, dusty dirt to make enough mud to cover the man's eyes. The Creator of the universe—the one who spoke the galaxies into existence and hurled the planets and electrons into orbit, the one who picked up dirt and made the human race—was bent over, staring at the hot ground and expectorating with all his might to bring hope, healing and redemption to one man.

It's a picture of a person who's willing to enter into the mess for the sake of community. The glory of God is displayed when the Son of God spits on the ground to restore sight and to restore a man to community.

Jesus didn't stop with the spitting. He also sweat for community and bled for community. On the night of his crucifixion, a night when he could have arguably and understandably been concerned about nothing beyond his own well-being, Jesus voiced a prayer to his Father that revealed his foremost thoughts and emotions. No, it's not the one about letting the cup of wrath and suffering pass from him. It's the prayer he prayed for his disciples. And for us.

> My prayer is not for them alone. I pray also for those who will believe in me through their message, that all of them may be one, Father, just as you are in me and I am in you. May they also be in us so that the world may believe that you have sent me. (Jn 17:20-21)

He sweat through his prayers that night.

Later he would bleed for community. At some point between 9:00 a.m. and 3:00 p.m., he hung on the cross, suspended between heaven and earth, and he looked down and noticed his friend John and his mother, Mary. "When Jesus saw his mother there, and the disciple whom he loved standing nearby, he said to her, 'Woman, here is your son,' and to the disciple, 'Here is your mother.' From that time on, this disciple took her into his home" (Jn 19:26-27).

Beaten by soldiers, hanging by threads of skin and muscle, bearing the weight of sin, rejected by his Father, Jesus instructed his mom and his friend to take care of one another. He knew that in three days they would see him again, but in the meantime, they would need the comfort of community. Even in the last moments of his life, Jesus was concerned about community. In fact, community is the very essence of his character. The complex doctrine of the Trinity demonstrates to us that God exists in community with himself. Scripture proclaims that God is love because he is inherently relational. And ultimately that's what he was dying for. To restore community. Between humankind and God. And within the mess of humankind itself.

He has now invited us into the mess. Jesus said we would be known as his disciples because of our love for one another. That love doesn't just happen passively or instinctively or by accident. We've got to bleed community. We've got to be willing to sweat for it. And we've got to be willing to get messy. The community of God is built by our blood, sweat and spit.

## The NCC Mess

The place where I'm currently bleeding, sweating and spitting is called National Community Church in Washington, D.C. We're a multisite church that meets in movie theaters, performance theaters and coffeehouses around the DC metro area. An eclectic collection of Capitol Hill staffers, artists, students, entrepreneurs, moms and dads, singles, Republicans, Democrats, homeless and wealthy (at least one or two of these are hard people to have community with), we believe the church belongs in the middle of the marketplace and should be the most creative place on the planet. If the kingdom of God were a

> **Spitting happens at National Community Church, especially on Heather's weekends to preach. Watch out, front row!**
>
> *MAEGAN HAWLEY*

business, our offices would be in the Research and Development Department. From now on, I'll probably just refer to our church the way the regulars do—"NCC."

My path toward ministry began at Epcot Center when I was in the seventh grade. That's right, the Environmental Prototype Community of Tomorrow, the nerd park of Disney World. (I still remember what the acronym stands for.) While riding the little boats in the Land Pavilion, I didn't realize that, as a middle-school kid, I was supposed to be completely bored and sulking to be on that stupid "ride" instead of on Space Mountain. Instead I was captivated by the joint research of Disney, NASA and the USDA to develop experimental life-support systems and sustainable agriculture for low-gravity environments. I had no idea what degree or job title I needed to do that kind of work, but I knew that's what I wanted to do.

Five years later, I found myself oscillating between the theater and engineering programs at various institutes of higher learning. Anchored by my Epcot experience, I made the logical decision and chose the career path that offered long-term opportunities and financial stability. I went to Louisiana State University to study biological engineering. That was the last time I made a decision based on common sense.

A bachelor's degree and master's degree later, I found myself in Washington, D.C., working for a U.S. senator on the Environment and Public Works Committee. Then I strayed over to Nashville for a few years to work in environmental consulting. Right after 9/11, I found myself back in DC again for another stint on Capitol Hill with environment and energy policy, and that's when the slow trick into ministry began. It's a pretty circuitous path, but Paul's journey to Rome was no less meandering. And maybe that's the first lesson: we bleed, sweat and spit sometimes because running after God can be a ride of bumps and whiplash.

The pages bound together in this book tell the tale of NCC's mess. It's about the things we're learning about living in community, becoming disciples and growing in our relationship with Christ in Washington, D.C. While your context is different, I hope there are a handful of things that might encourage you, spark new ideas or be beneficial in your environment too. I've tried to separate principles from practical applications, focus on the principles and specify when I'm speaking descriptively and not prescriptively, but sometimes it all gets messed up together.

## The Cheat Sheet

Before I go further, I thought it might be helpful to provide you with a list of terms and teams that will pop up over and over again in this text. I always define and describe them the first time they're mentioned, but it's hard to retain all that stuff as you're reading. Not to mention the fact that you may only read the chapters that look relevant to your situation. So, you can use this for reference.

**National Community Church (NCC).** A multisite church in Washington, D.C., where I serve as a discipleship pastor.

**Team D.** The discipleship team at National Community Church, which is responsible for helping me lead small groups and develop churchwide discipleship initiatives.

**The Hungry Mothers.** A group of girls I met at my first small group in DC who became fast friends over chips and salsa. Leslie, Christy and Ruth are my accountability, my sanity, my encouragers and my personal butt kickers every now and then.

> **Team D isn't really *that* responsible. I jumped Will's car, and on the same day, Heather's Saturn went out of orbit (a.k.a., ran out of gas). Classic Team D.**
>
> *MAEGAN HAWLEY*

**The Gang.** The crew of friends that my husband Ryan and I have known the longest in DC. When we think of the people who've most shaped our lives and whom we trust the most, it's the people in The Gang.

**Will Johnston and Maegan Hawley.** Team D members at NCC. Their sidebar comments run throughout the book.

**Ryan Zempel (or most often simply "Ryan").** My amazing husband, whom I met in a small group over a decade ago at NCC.

# Community Is Messy

*Anything you build on a large scale or with intense passion invites chaos.*

**FRANCIS FORD COPPOLA**

**C**ommunity is great. Once upon a time, we small group leaders heard a pastor give a stirring message on the theological, ecclesiological and practical importance of life in community, and we left with a newfound conviction that we needed to get involved. An announcement was made from the pulpit about the need for new small group leaders, so we decided to put our convictions into practice because we were convinced both spiritually and experientially that small groups are great. We courageously attended leadership training classes and left with a passion to change the world through the greatness of small groups. The church promoted our small group in print, in words and in pictures, and we approached the night of our first meeting with holy anticipation. Because small groups are great.

And then the people showed up.

Community is great until you actually experience it. It might not happen on the first night, in the first month or even in the first year, but at some point, our well-tended community falls apart. The chairs are set, the snacks are ready, the lesson is prepared, the service project is planned, and you're doing everything you need to do as a leader. Then, all of a sudden, you realize there were some things no one ever told you about leading small groups. The nice thoughts about growth and friends and transparency and community tricked you into leadership, but there were a few things that went unmentioned in leadership training. You have just discovered that community is messy.

Community is messy because it always involves people, and people are messy. It's about people hauling their brokenness and baggage into your house and dumping it in your living room.

What do you do at that moment? The moment you realize that the people you've committed your life to are messy becomes the defining moment of your leadership.

## Biblical Mess

We have a long and notoriously messy history as the people of God. Let's go all the way back to the beginning. God created, and everything was good, but we didn't last three chapters before we messed it up. Eve disobeyed God, encouraged Adam to join in the mess, and sin mess happened. Fingers got pointed, and relational mess happened. The inevitable results of sin were pronounced, and life mess ensued.

The story continues to the next generation with Cain and Abel. I would say jealousy and murder amount to mess. Noah built a huge boat to house representatives from every species. I can't imagine that was the cleanest environment. Afterward, this great and noble hero of the faith got himself drunk, and his sons discovered him naked. Mess.

Then there was Abraham claiming that his wife was not his wife and navigating water resources rights with his nephew as their herdsmen fought over the best plots of land. We find Isaac and Rebekah playing favorites with their sons Jacob and Esau, which produced generations-long sibling rivalry. The story continues with Jacob showing favoritism to his son Joseph, which resulted in a family meltdown.

Fast-forward a few hundred years to Moses. I like to think of Moses as the first small group leader in the Bible. You thought your group was rough? Look at the people he was charged with leading. They couldn't follow instructions, complained incessantly and forgot the miracles they had seen in a matter of hours. While the Egyptians were plagued with lice and locusts, the Hebrews were plagued with attention deficit disorder.

Fast-forward a bit more to David. He was the second great small-group leader in the Bible. In 1 Samuel 22, we read that David was running for his life and decided to hide out in the cave of Adullam, where he was soon joined by his family. Maybe that was comforting to him, but I'm sure there are at least a few members of some families who wouldn't necessarily be the most comforting allies. Then, Scripture tells us, more reinforcements arrived as he was joined by men who were in trouble, in debt or just discontented. Great. Those are exactly the kind of people I want to show up to help me in my distress. How many of us feel like that's our small group? David's experience with messy relationships didn't end there; it was only the beginning. David and Saul, David and Uriah, David and Bathsheba, David and the prophet Nathan, David and his son Absalom. Okay, pretty much David and everyone.

Keep moving to the New Testament. Jesus was born in the mess of a stable—most likely a cave where animals were kept and fed—and placed in a stone feeding trough for animals. When he grew up, he called twelve men to follow him—fishermen, tax collectors, political revolutionaries—who bickered over who was going to be greatest in the kingdom.

In Acts 15, the apostles had to meet in Jerusalem to sort out a theological mess. Paul and Peter bickered, Paul and John Mark parted ways, and Paul and James disagreed on the interaction between faith and works. In fact, the majority of writings in the New Testament exist because the early church was messy. Let's consider the church at Corinth as a case study: incestuous affairs, lawsuits, divorce and separation, idol worship, big egos, doctrinal infighting, sexual promiscuity and people getting drunk while celebrating Communion. You know you've got a problem in your church when people are getting drunk on Communion. I feel obligated to point out that this obviously happened before we started using the plastic shot glasses of grape juice.

And you thought your small group was messed up.

## Standing in Cathedrals in Conflict

As we step further into the pages of church history, we find even more mess. Our history as the people of God is riddled with inconsistencies, heresies, hypocrisies and general stupidity. We launched inquisitions, crusades and systematic killings in the name of Christ. Peter and Paul, who lectured those who were healed under their ministry to worship Jesus alone, are now venerated by some to the point that they may once again be confused for deity.

I recently went on a pilgrimage following the footsteps of Paul in Greece and Italy, and I was reminded once again of our cluttered history as the people of God. There were many significant experiences, but one in particular reminded me of the mess of our story as the church. Standing in St. Peter's Basilica was a holy moment. Everything about the architecture and the art pointed me to Christ and gave me a window into the awe and wonder and majesty of God Almighty. It made me appreciate my connection to the thousands and thousands who came before me. I felt a sense of community with the saints and martyrs to whom I'm connected in the family of God. My stomach was in my throat.

Then something was triggered in the recesses of my Protestant brain—an incessant banging as on the door of the Castle Church in Wittenberg, Germany. I remembered that the construction of this magnificent basilica was facilitated in part by the sale of indulgences. My stomach turned. Tension. Conflict. Was this a moment when I was supposed to be enraptured by the glory of God? Or disgusted by the way his gospel had been perverted by people? Was this an opportunity to worship? Or an opportunity to walk out in protest?

While standing in cathedrals in conflict, I settled somewhere in the uncomfortable but inevitable land of the in-between and thanked God for his grace and sovereignty. I think that's what it boils down to. God is full of grace. God is sovereign. So even though we've been stupid along the way, his story moves forward and he builds his church through the mess.

The reality is that we're still constructing cultural hurdles to hold people at a distance and make it difficult for them to come into the presence of God. We still sell salvation; we just frame it differently—like promises of blessing in exchange for a donation to a televangelist. To be sure, future generations will look quizzically at our ecclesiology and wonder how the truth was ever able to prevail underneath the layers of bizarre faith practices.

But that's the beauty of our faith. It isn't up to us. It's all about God, his grace and his sovereignty. As we read stories from the pages of Scripture and the pens of the saints, we see the hand of God writing his own story in them and through them. Emerging from the mess is the fingerprint of God writing the hope of the gospel and the story of redemption.

The scary news? Community is messy. It always has been and always will be. Messy community is not the exception to the rule; it's the rule. The good news is that mess, when engaged rightly, can be the very thing that brings what we most want in groups: community and growth.

Proverbs 14:4 has become one of my organizing metaphors in regard to community, church, small groups or whatever circles of mess we find ourselves in: "Where there are no oxen, the manger is empty, but from the strength of an ox come abundant harvests."

You can have a clean barn with no animals in it, but you aren't going to get much done without animals. Likewise, you can have a tidy church as long as no one is in it, but community requires that we show up. And showing up means bringing our mess.

## Pig Lagoons

I learned an important lesson at a pig farm about dealing with mess. When I was a graduate student in the biological engineering department at Louisiana State University, I took a class called Bioreactor Design. You know, the standard preparatory path to ministry. Anyway, bioreactors are used to grow cells and tissues; they're systems that transform raw materials into useful products. The class focused on understanding the variables and catalysts of the reactions that transformed raw inputs into productive outputs—like turning chemicals into medicines and wastewater into wetlands. It was about designing a system in which transformation was catalyzed.

Toward the end of the semester, each of us was required to participate in a research project. While most of my classmates were designing systems that allowed them to work with snazzy laboratory equipment or were studying reaction kinetics for cranking out pharmaceuticals, I was sloshing through the mud and poop of Ben Hur Research Farm every day to take samples from the treatment lagoon at the pig feeding operation. And when I say poop, I mean literal poop; that's not a metaphor for mess.

Here's the deal. Pig farms stink. I mean, they stink really badly. In Louisiana, there were laws that regulated how bad the stink could be. Imagine a day in mid-July when the thermometer reads ninety-five and the humidity is 195 percent. On a day like that, you just don't want the stink to be any worse than it has to be. Most of the farmers dealt with the poop by washing down the animal pens and discharging all the sludge to a treatment lagoon, and my goal was to reduce the stink. That required me to determine the kinetic parameters for the reactions in the lagoon that broke down the waste and converted it into useful product—fertilizer—and to come up with new lagoon designs that maximized those reactions. Reducing the stink meant looking at the variables that most impacted the transformation and maximizing those in the design of the environment. Clear as sludge?

Basically all the pig poop gets washed into this lagoon . . . and I've got to make it less stinky. Here's what I learned. On one hand, I couldn't just turn a blind eye (or in this case, a clogged nostril) to the stink and pretend it didn't exist. I couldn't just wish it away or will it away. On the other hand, I couldn't do anything directly about the stink. I couldn't hover over the lagoon, raise my Moses staff and command the stink to be gone. There was no miracle formula I could drop into the lagoon to make the stink disappear. There was no way to attack the stink directly.

Instead I had to focus on creating an environment in which the stink was most effectively and efficiently converted into a useful and beneficial product. The point was not to focus on the stink but to focus on the environment—to design an environment that fostered change and maximized transformation.

The title of my final report was "Determination of Kinetic Parameters of Swine Waste under Anoxic Conditions." I barely even understand what that means anymore, but the point was transforming mess into something good.

In the church, the stink takes the form of sin, circumstances, conflict, personality differences, teenagers, deacons—the "whatever" we perceive to be inhibiting growth and community. Sometimes we try to ignore it, hoping that time and inertia will be our ally and one day the stink will no longer exist. Or we try to deal with the stink directly. We think if we point at it and say, "Stop!" firmly enough, it will go away. We hope that if we preach hard enough or pray loud enough the problem will die, and the stink will dissipate. The result is that mess might be ignored or hidden, but nothing changes. Neither ignoring the mess nor halfway dealing with it in a roundabout way brings lasting transformation.

In reality, we need to approach things like my bioreactor design class did: acknowledge that crap is a natural byproduct of life, and work to create environments that catalyze change.

## Mess and Growth: There Is Always a Link

I've discovered the hard way, and I'm beginning to discover in a hopeful way, that mess and transformation are directly proportional. There's always a link.

I live in a world where mess abounds. My church is about 60 percent single, and about 75 percent are in their twenties and thirties. Many of them work jobs that have political overtones or undertones. The three issues I find myself addressing more than any others are how to have appropriate relational and sexual boundaries, how to approach alcohol biblically and responsibly, and how to navigate tricky political issues with people whose passions and jobs are fueled by them.

Sometimes mess is the byproduct of growth. Even when things are working properly, there will still be a messy byproduct. For example, if a car is running, there will be exhaust. Several years ago, a young man in our church attended a leadership training class that focused on the need for transparency among leaders. He decided to put that into practice, which meant he needed to confess to a pastor that he struggled with same-sex attraction. The growth in his life (a desire to be more transparent) resulted in a messy byproduct (a confession that had to be engaged by the pastor). That young man grew through the mess and today serves as a sought-after advisor in our group ministry.

Sometimes it works the other way around: mess can be the catalyst for change. Mess happens, and it causes people to grow as a result. Think about compost piles. They don't do their job unless trash is heaped on them regularly. A few years ago, a leader met with me to let me know he was stepping down from leadership and submitting to spiritual authority for correction and discipline. He confessed that he had been hanging out with his small group one night and had a bit too much to drink. The result was behavior inappropriate for a Christ-follower, much less for a leader. He submitted to a process of accountability that catalyzed spiritual growth in his life with the result that his transparency and response actually caused those around him to respect him more. He later served as a coach in our small group ministry.

Whether mess is the byproduct or the catalyst, it's often an important variable in the environment of transformation. Mess means that change is happening, is right around the corner or will happen if we engage it correctly.

Categories always seem to break down and bleed into one another. There are sin messes, relational messes and life messes, but those lines often blur. A sin mess can lead to a relational mess or a life mess, and vice versa. An issue that starts as a life mess can break down into relational mess or sin mess. And since categories, though limiting, can be helpful to us as we think strategically about how to respond to messes, let's consider them.

*Sin messes.* These don't necessarily happen within the context of a group meeting or experience; sometimes they occur between an individual and God. But the effects of sin still create messes in groups. We encounter sin messes when we discover someone in our group is having an affair, engaging in unethical business practices, or struggling with an addiction or some other destructive habit.

Several years ago I led a small group that I was convinced was the most perfect group God ever put together. I couldn't believe it—it was full of young, smart, likable, energetic and attractive twenty-somethings who seemed eager and hungry to grow in their relationships with God. We had great discussions about the Bible and experienced great community life throughout the week. I was convinced God could change the world through us.

Until I got a phone call from my coleader. He prefaced the conversation with "Are you sitting down?" and proceeded to tell me that two single individuals in the group—one of whom we were raising up as a potential leader—were sleeping together. In fact, they had been living together. That was just the beginning. As we began to walk through that, we discovered sin messes in the lives of other group members as well. And I even had to come face-to-face with a few of my own.

James 5:16 tells us we should confess our sins to one another, not to receive forgiveness as much as to receive healing. Walking through sin together builds our character, takes us one step in the direction of restoring us to the people God created us to be and helps us look more like Christ.

*Relational messes.* In group life, we encounter this second type of mess most often. It's the kind that happens between two individuals. Or three. Or four. Or among everyone in the group. It includes the talking messes—you know what I'm talking about, right? Long talkers, no talkers, off-topic talkers, narcissistic talkers, extra-grace-required talkers, theologically divisive talkers, weird talkers, trash talkers. It's also the mess of conflict or disagreement or personality clashes. It's the mess of agreeing to agree on doctrine and agreeing to disagree over opinion, only to learn that you disagree over what's doctrine and what's opinion. Or maybe it happens on your leadership team as different people hold to different opinions about how a task should be performed. Basically it's the mess that predictably and inevitably happens whenever you put more than one person in a room together.

Let me tell you a little story about my good buddy John Hasler and me. John worked with me on Team D (that's what we affectionately call the discipleship team at NCC) for several years. We love each other, learn from each other and have shared many, many laughs. But let's just say that some of our opinions are as different as the gulf that separates the elephants from the donkeys in this city. In summary, I come from a flag-waving, July 4th-celebrating, military family from the South. John is . . . I don't even know how to describe him. He would disagree with whatever label I try to put on him anyway. Let's just say the first argument we had came about because I used the word *patriotism*, naively thinking everyone considered that to be a positive thing.

Several months ago, John and I were working on a fairly large and significant churchwide initiative that required lots of caffeine, many offsite brainstorming meetings and regular intellectually challenging conversations. I'd love to report that every time we worked on this project we saw the Shekinah glory, felt

the overwhelming presence of God and heard the inaudible but
unmistakable voice of God. That happened once or twice. But
usually it was just hard-core, gut-it-out work. On a few occa-
sions, it was pretty grueling and even downright frustrating.

One day in particular stands out. John and I had spent an
entire afternoon hashing through things until we were completely exhausted mentally and emotionally. Driving back to
the office, we erupted into a heated discussion as we passed the
Lincoln Memorial. *About* the Lincoln Memorial. Yes, about it.
John made an "observation" about how sad that good ole
Christian Abe Lincoln must be about being enshrined in a
pagan temple forever. I gave out a long, exasperated sigh in my
heart, but I remained calm on the outside. "John, I don't think
he's really in a pagan temple."

John retorted, "Of course it is. It's modeled after the Parthenon."

My exasperation started to make its appearance. "Well,
yeah. It was an architectural decision. That's what was popular
at the time."

John: "It's still a pagan temple."

Me: "Well, then everything in this city is a pagan temple,
because everything is based on that architectural aesthetic."

John: "Exactly. I'm just not sure that Lincoln would appreciate that for his monument."

Me (exasperation fully unleashed): "John, seriously, it's not
like people are going there to worship."

John (replying under his breath): "Huh. I'm not so sure about
that."

Then full-scale ridiculous argumentation ensued until I col-
lected myself and decided to be the adult. Calmly I said, "John,
let's be reasonable about this. I don't think any of the designers
or builders ever intended for anyone to think of the Lincoln
Memorial as a temple."

That's the moment when John reminded me of the inscription above the memorial: "In this temple as in the hearts of the people for whom he saved the Union the memory of Abraham Lincoln is enshrined forever."

Oops.

This isn't the only relational mess John and I have stumbled into. We've explored all kinds of relational messes together. And by the way, when we returned to the office, I couldn't help but point out his wall calendar from Greece. That thing was covered with legit pagan temples. His last-resort excuse: "My mom gave that to me."

While walking through

> **Heather really hates to lose arguments, so this irrelevant paragraph is her attempt to get the last word. But really, John beat her fair, square and solidly.**
>
> **WILL JOHNSTON**

sin mess heals us, restores us and grows our character, walking through relational mess forces us to grow in our obedience of the "one another" commands. There are about fifty of these in Scripture, and they can't be obeyed outside the context of community—love one another, serve one another, honor one another, forgive one another, encourage one another, confess to one another. These commands move us past small talk and illusions of friendship to the messiness of biblical community.

*Life messes.* Life mess isn't connected to insidious sin or inevitable personality differences. It's the kind of mess that happens because we live in a fallen world. Think sudden death, divorce, cancer, a job loss. These don't necessarily happen within the context of your group or because of your group, but they still affect your group. When the body of Christ lives as it should, the whole group suffers when one member suffers.

Life messes happen in our groups here on Capitol Hill at

least every two years. Sometimes a group contains people on both the left side and the right side of the political aisle, and the election cycle can mean significant change simultaneously for all of them. Some lose jobs while others earn promotions. Paul says we should rejoice with those who rejoice and mourn with those who mourn, and I often find myself doing both on the same day every couple of years. It's a challenge for a leader to rejoice with those whose lives are changing for the good and to mourn simultaneously with those who face loss.

Joseph's response to his brothers in Genesis 50:20 is instructive: "You intended to harm me, but God intended it for good." Joseph had been the victim of sin mess, relational mess *and* life mess. Because he chose to respond to these messy moments in his life with integrity and humility, God used them to propel him into his calling, and his response to his brothers reveals an attitude toward mess that's a great example for us to follow. The fact that we're in a mess and the circumstances surrounding the mess aren't really the issue; the issue is how we grow because we're there.

Mess happens. It's the rule, and it can be a good thing.

## Engineers and Inspectors

Okay, enough buildup. We've come to the moment when I'm supposed to give you the solution. Bad news: there isn't one. I have no idea how to address the mess you're facing in your community. There's no formula for dealing with a mess, because every mess is different, every leader is different, and the variables at play in any given situation are endless.

Instead of recommending a formula, let me suggest a posture: be an engineer, not a compliance inspector.

In my engineering world, there were two kinds of people: the engineers who worked on behalf of companies to ensure everything operated smoothly, efficiently and productively; and their nemeses, the inspectors, who were often employed by the government to burden us with rules and bury us under paperwork. Compliance inspectors conduct audits and tell you what's wrong. It's easy to point out messes and deliver opinions; it's much harder to create environments where the mess can be transformed.

Compliance inspectors focus on the problem; engineers focus on the solution. Compliance inspectors care most about outputs; engineers care most about inputs. Compliance inspectors write reports on how well you're following the rules; engineers draw up plans for making environments better.

Engineers look for solutions, and as a small group leader or a ministry leader, you're an environmental engineer—you're creating environments that foster spiritual growth.

It's not the leader's job to eliminate and eradicate mess from a small group; that's the Hoy Spirit's job. Your job as a leader is to create an environment in which people can best see, respond to and engage in the work of the Holy Spirit. Your job is to engineer an environment where transformation can happen. What comes next isn't a formula, flow chart or step-by-step instruction manual. I'm not even sure I would call it best practices. It's just a list of a few things that are helping me navigate mess.

*1. Acknowledge the mess.* Let's just acknowledge mess when it happens and not be afraid to call it what it is. Paul told the church of Philippi, "I plead with Euodia and I plead with Syntyche to be of the same mind in the Lord" (Phil 4:2). Imagine being one of them when that letter was read out loud to the entire congregation. I have no idea what those two women were arguing about, but they are forever remembered as the women who had to be scolded publicly by Paul.

When mess happens, admit it. Even self-help programs recognize that the first step toward any change is to admit there's a problem. Acknowledging the mess invites accountability, expresses recognition that change must happen and moves us one step toward that change. Don't let an elephant linger in the room. Stating clearly that a mess exists also allows everyone involved to breathe a little easier, since everyone knew about it, but no one was talking about it.

**2. Identify the kind of mess.** It might help to identify the kind of mess you're encountering. Is it a sin mess? A relational mess? A life mess? Often it's a combination of two or maybe even all three. Once we've identified it, we can think more clearly about how to address it. Sin messes might need to be cleaned—like hazardous waste spills. Relational messes need to be navigated. Life messes need to be tended—to be cared for. Identifying the kind of mess may keep you from feeling immediately overwhelmed.

**3. Have the right perspective.** Mess isn't the end of community life; it could be the catalyst for the kind of community you hope to see. Sometimes you have to take a big step back to see the bigger picture. I believe our perspective makes all the difference.

I talk about metaphors from the engineering world quite a bit, so let me shift gears and give you an illustration from the art world. I checked off a life goal recently at the Art Institute of Chicago when I viewed one of my favorite paintings in person for the first time—Seurat's *Sunday Afternoon on the Island of La Grande Jatte*. That reminds me of a conversation from another piece of critically acclaimed art—the movie *Clueless*. When the character Tai asked, "What's a Monet?" the budding art historian Cher responded, "It's like a painting, see? From far away, it's okay, but up close, it's a big old mess."

Seurat followed the Impressionists with a twist on their form—what came to be called pointillism or neo-impressionism. Close up, it's exactly as Cher described it. A mess. Random dots.

But if you back up, you see its true design.

Seurat experimented at the crossroads of art and science. He attempted to paint dots in such a way that the eye would blend them, resulting in more vibrant tones and dynamic images. The result? The human eye sees colors that aren't actually on the canvas itself. A masterpiece emerges from the mess, but you need the right perspective to see it.

Sometimes you have to take a big step back to see God's perspective on what's happening in your group. Perspective can transform the mess of our lives into a masterpiece of God's transforming power. If you're like me, you have a tendency to see everything that happens in your group—both good and bad—as a reflection of your leadership. When sin, conflict or bad things happen to members, my immediate instinct is to assume narcissistically that something is wrong with my leadership. When the sin mess that eventually turned into relational mess happened in my group, I immediately thought, *What did I do wrong?*

Now, I think looking at your leadership is always a good thing. I did plenty of things wrong in that group. But sometimes it's not a matter of "what did I do wrong?" but of "what did I do right?" Sin happens. Conflict happens. Life happens. Mess happens. People don't necessarily sin or get into petty arguments because you're a bad leader. It could be that you're a great leader who has created a safe environment in which God can bring those things to the surface to deal with them.

You see, those small group members sleeping together wasn't a problem with my leadership. There were deeply rooted issues that went back further than my friendship, and our group provided a place where God could bring the issues to light and surgically begin to bring conviction, repentance, healing and hope. When mess happens, you might be exactly where God wants you to be as a group. The question is, what does he want to do and how does he want to work?

My friend and pastor, Mark Batterson, challenges me with this statement: "All of us love miracles right? We just don't like finding ourselves in situations where we need a miracle. But that is a prerequisite."[1]

Messes are incubators for miracles.

*4. Ask good questions.* In every mess you face, there's what you know and there's reality. Between the two, a vast chasm often exists. Suspend judgment and fill the void of what's known and what's reality with good questions. Asking good questions allows you to go beneath the surface mess and discover the roots of the mess. On the surface, we may see a relational mess, but as we dig deeper, we may discover there's a sin mess lurking beneath the surface. Or maybe we're dealing with what we think is a relational mess, but a few good questions reveals that the bitterness or the envy is actually the rotten fruit of a life mess. Every situation is unique and requires a different approach, but here are some questions you can ask as a leader that might be helpful:

- What's the most difficult situation you're facing right now?

- How do difficulties in your personal life affect the way you relate to other people?

- How might your life be different if you were to find a way to resolve this mess?

- What's one thing you wish I knew about you? What's one thing you wish everyone in the group knew about you? What's one thing you wish you knew about everyone in the group?

- I've noticed that people tend to—pick one of the following: respond negatively to certain people, always show up late for group, rarely enter into the conversation, monopolize the conversation, get defensive—during group. What's going on there? How would your group experience look different if members didn't respond in these ways?

*5. Talk to the right people.* Know where you can go for support, guidance and assistance. There's a big difference between getting help and spreading gossip, so make sure you're going to people who can actually come alongside you to help you clean, navigate or tend the mess. Who is a coach, a pastor or a trusted friend who can help you know how to engage the mess?

It's important to acknowledge that some messes require professional counseling. One of the best leadership decisions you may ever make is to recognize that you're not the best leader for every situation. When your small group begins to revolve around the mess of one person, the mess has become toxic and requires professional attention. You don't just stand around and watch a hazardous waste spill and hope it will clean itself. You call in professionals. Coaches and counselors are your friends. Know where to find them and how to use them.

*6. Communicate a biblical goal.* No mess is fatal. If a leader has failed and it requires him or her to step out of leadership, look forward to the day when that person will be able to step back into a position of responsibility and authority. When I encounter messes—as a leader, a third-party observer or an instigator—I try to ask myself two questions: (1) How do we all grow from this? (2) How might God want to get glory from this?

Those seem to be the two primary ways God brings beauty out of mess—by helping us grow and by getting glory in the midst of it. People like Moses, Joseph, David and Peter were all given places of authority but were also required to go through a season of growth and refinement before they entered into the place of maximum influence.

How do we all grow? That's the ultimate goal, after all. When mess happens, I often address this question to everyone—not just those directly involved in the mess. How do we grow as the body of Christ? How do I grow as a leader? How do you grow as participants? How do we all grow as a group? Recognizing that there are growth opportunities for all of us fuels a sense of belonging and a need for one another. It helps us recognize that we're all sons and daughters of God who need to mature.

How might God want to get glory? If we look to Scripture as the script for our own stories, we can be encouraged that God gets glory in spite of and sometimes because of our messes. Wondering how God might get glory out of a mess sparks holy imagination and inspires hope that all is not lost and all is not meaningless. Even if the mess doesn't completely resolve, we can always learn something, we can always grow, and God can still glorify himself in the midst of it.

*7. Commit to the process.* Finally, commit to the process. Walking through messes requires transparency, commitment to people, leadership, care, time, prayer, discernment and digging into the Word. The question is, are you willing to fight? Not fight the mess, but fight in the midst of messy environments to become the answer to Jesus' prayer that his followers be one (Jn 17:20-21)? Are we committed to fight for the unity and the community that Christ prayed for on the night of his crucifixion? Are we committed to fight through the mess to fulfill his command to make disciples in our generation?

## Final Apologetic

Some of us live on the verge of giving up because we're tired from carrying the mess. We reconsider our leadership, question the point of community and grow tired of the stink. I want to encourage you to hold your nose and hold on, because you're engaged in the greatest mission of history. When Jesus gave his last command, the Great Commission, he said, "Go and make disciples of all nations." He didn't say go *find* disciples. He said go *make* disciples. That means it's work. And that requires us to embrace and enter into the mess.

Jesus was willing to get down into the mess of life. He touched lepers, befriended despised people and hung out with notorious sinners. He was willing to enter into the kind of community that requires our blood, sweat and spit.

Let's go back to the prayer that Jesus prayed on the night of his betrayal and crucifixion, in which he expressed his desire that all his disciples would be "one" (Jn 17:20-21). He didn't pray they would be one just for the sake of community, but so that "the world will know."

Author and theologian Francis Schaeffer made this observation:

> Jesus goes on in this 21st verse to say something that always causes me to cringe. If as Christians we do not cringe, it seems to me we're not very sensitive or very honest, because Jesus here gives us the final apologetic. What is the final apologetic? "That all of them may be one, Father, just as you are in me and I am in you. May they also be in us so that the world may believe that you have sent me." This is the final apologetic.[2]

Apologetics is a branch of theology concerned with the defense of the Christian faith, and we often think of it in terms of defending the historicity and truthfulness of Scripture. But Schaeffer makes a statement that moves apologetics from the cerebral to the practical. He states that we—the family of God, the body of Christ, the church, the community that we experience—should be the ultimate and final proof for God. We can look at scientific evidence, historical evidence, literary evidence and archaeological evidence and build proof after proof after proof to defend our beliefs. But at the end of the day, the definitive proof is in the way we relate to one another. That's the final apologetic.

It's not a new idea. Jesus told his disciples, "A new command I give you: Love one another. As I have loved you, so you must love one another. By this everyone will know that you are my disciples, if you love one another" (Jn 13:34-35).

When was the last time you and your circle of friends were accused of being Christians because your love for one another was so intense?

Community is great. And then the people show up. When people show up, a group becomes the place where mess happens. But that mess may prove to be the answer to our prayers. It may become the catalyst for, the byproduct of and the environment in which discipleship happens. We move from a great program to the body of Christ, and we become the body of Christ broken and battered and bloodied and poured out for those around us. The body of Christ where community and redemption are found.

# Everything Is an Experiment

*All life is an experiment. The more experiments you make the better.*

**RALPH WALDO EMERSON**

Labs are great places to make messes, because you can blow things up and make poisonous gases and do all kinds of crazy stuff in an environment that isn't fatal. There are drains and hoods and eye showers. Labs are safe places to make a big mess, because you can contain failure. But most importantly they're places to make discoveries.

In 1996, I was in the final days of completing my course requirements, papers and projects for my biological engineering degree. The final test was a senior design project that the department masterminds had crafted to bring all of our newly discovered engineering expertise to bear on the design, construction, testing and performance analysis of an engineering system. I decided to design and build an aquaponics system—a technology that combines traditional aquaculture (producing fish in a confined and controlled environment) and hydroponics (growing vegetables with nutrient-rich water). My particular aquaponics system featured tomato plants on top of a tilapia fish tank.

The idea was that tomatoes would benefit the fish system by removing some of the solid waste from their environment, and the fish system would benefit the tomatoes by providing them with fertilizing nutrients. The biggest win was the delivery of two marketable products off the same limited land mass and system. That might not seem like a big deal, but in urban environments with limited space, third world countries with limited resources and arid climates with limited rainfall, it's a really cool idea.

The experiment was going great. *Really* great. I was receiving high marks and was well on my way to the top grade in the class. As graduation day neared, I completed the final paperwork for graduate studies and plotted my potential thesis research around this system. Somebody from Disney's Epcot Center even expressed interest in the project. This was more than an experiment; this was my launch to nerd fame.

The day of my final presentation came, and the room was packed with students and professors who were excited to hear more about my project. It went great. Well, except for the moment that the computers crashed and killed my PowerPoint; my entire presentation of data, charts and graphs disappeared. But I just hauled people into the lab to give our presentation at the fish tanks. It was a big win. People who were unfamiliar with the project got a great visual, and I didn't have to endure nitpicky questions about individual data points on our linear regressions and other statistical analysis.

But then . . . The next day I walked into what appeared to be a scene from *Fishpacolypse Now*. Dead fish everywhere. They had escaped the tank and jumped onto the floor. Some had breathed their last while lounging on my tomato pads. A few unfortunate creatures that had made a brave attempt to escape through the PVC pipes were mangled in them. I checked a few things before running back to class—the pH, the temperature, the dissolved oxygen levels. No, I didn't check the dissolved oxygen levels. I just heard . . . nothing.

The lab was eerily quiet, and that's when I realized quiet was a problem. And that's when everything went into slow motion. When I had gone into the lab the day before, my friend Jonathan had turned off the oxygen so the audience could hear the presentation better. An hour later, the presentation was complete. After the formal handshakes with the committee and hugs and high fives with friends, I left the lab to celebrate, forgetting to resume the flow of oxygen into the tank.

While I was gasping in celebratory laughter with my friends, those poor fish were gasping for air in an oxygen-depleted environment and heading into the most exhausting night of their lives. And for some of them, it would be their last. The apostle Peter caught 153 fish in one day. I killed about one hundred.

I created a mess in a lab in order to experiment with emerging technologies and discover new solutions to old problems. In the church, we are likewise faced with old problems, but the ways we help people navigate those are in constant need of evaluation and experimentation. Scripture seems to indicate that God was a fan of experiments from the beginning.

## The Divine Lab

When God said, "Let there be light," he opened the lab of the universe. He distributed galaxies into empty space and flung planets into orbit, hung burning balls of gas to light up the blackness of the sky, and on Planet Earth, he opened his divine lab. On the spherical firmament orbiting the star called the sun, mountains sprung high and waters covered the surface. Birds flew in the sky, fish swam in the sea, insects crawled on the ground, and dinosaurs thundered across the land. And God said it was good.

Against this canvas, he began to write his story. And while we can be confident of the ending, we live according to the pen of an author who never writes the same story twice. Every plot line is infused with a new twist.

If the children of Israel had expected God to win their battles for the Promised Land the same way every time, they would have constantly looked for a giant body of water to swallow the enemy army. Or they would have marched around all the cities for seven days in hopes of seeing the walls come down. Instead they discovered that God performed miracles in different ways at different times to display different dimensions of his character. And if they were to be successful, they had to wait on and be obedient to his specific commands in each situation.

Jesus showed great creative latitude in the way he healed people. Sometimes he healed them because of their faith. Other times he healed them because of their friends' faith. Once he spit into the ground and made mud balls to heal a blind man. There were moments when he laid hands on people and other moments where he just spoke a word. One healing seemed to happen without his full awareness . . . or was he purposefully provoking the woman who touched his robe?

Jesus' method of discipleship changed from person to person and situation to situation. He used a variety of experiences, conversations and relationships to relay his message. He taught, performed miracles, asked provocative questions and even engaged in riddles and mockery to help people discover truth.

Jesus also enlisted his disciples in his evangelism experiments, sending the seventy out to heal the sick and cast out demons. Sometimes they were successful. Other times they weren't.

When Jesus said, "Go make disciples of all nations" (Mt 28:19), he initiated an experiment of discipleship that continues to play out in the lab of history today. As we look at our history as the community of God, we find that revolutions, revivals and reformations were fueled by innovation and creativity. The kingdom of God has been built on a series of daring and divine experiments.

## Shiny Pennies

There's more than one way to make a penny shiny. Here's a real-life example of a challenge that the National Community Church staff had to find a solution to.

*Pop Quiz*

We need to distribute four thousand shiny pennies to our congregation. The U.S. Mint won't give us new ones, so we have to get grubby old pennies from the bank and figure out a way to restore their shine. What common household chemical should we use to reverse the chemical oxidation?

  a. Vinegar and salt
  b. Ketchup
  c. Lemon juice

The answer? All of the above. All of them work because they are all acidic. There are ways of making pennies shiny that perhaps you had not thought of yet. The underlying chemical principles remain the same, but the way it's carried out is different. Don't confuse goals with methods. There's more than one way to make a bad penny shine.

Likewise, is it possible there's more than one way to make a disciple?

At NCC, we have a core value called "Everything is an experiment." We celebrate the idea that there are lots of different kinds of churches because there are lots of different kinds of people, and we often claim that we're part of the Research and

Development Department of the body of Christ. We believe
there are ways of "doing" church that no one has thought of yet,
and that conviction trickles into our views of community and
discipleship. Maybe there are ways of creating community and
making disciples for our generation to discover. We are willing
to take risks because we believe with all our hearts that the
greatest risk is to take no risk at all.

Let's go back to the fish slaughter for a moment. New technologies require tremendous attention to the variables that
affect them, and when you're dealing with biological systems,
the stakes are even higher. One small change in an environmental condition can significantly affect the entire system.
Today we're facing a changing culture and an emerging generation that interacts with its environment differently than an
generation before it. It's influenced by the cultural trends and
the changing face of communities ranging from Facebook to
Twitter. How do we design and maintain an environment for
biblical growth for emerging generations? We roll up our sleeves,
step into the lab and do some creative experimentation.

## Free-Market Small Group Philosophy

When Jesus said, "Go make disciples," he launched us into one
of the most challenging experiments of history. At NCC, we
view every small group as a discipleship experiment. If you had
to classify our model according to standard group-life termi-
nology, we're "free market" in our approach. Free-market small-
group systems allow for a high degree of relational connection
and creativity by allowing leaders to turn their existing relationships, gifts, interests, passions and hobbies into disciple-
making small groups.

Jesus never seemed to heal, teach or motivate the same way
twice. He was the master of creating unique experiences and

sparking targeted conversations for tailor-made discipleship experiences. So why do churches force people into little clusters that all look alike, slap the label "small group" on them and then promise that the participants will grow exponentially in their faith as a result?

For any small group or discipleship program to be successful, we need leaders who burn white hot with a vision for making disciples. That's why we implement a free-market small group system at NCC: we believe discipleship happens best within the context of shared interests, and it flows naturally out of leaders who are driven by a passionate vision from God.

It's tempting for me to just dream up a vision, build a structure to support that vision and then ask leaders to serve that vision. I'd love to create a one-size-fits-all approach to discipleship, roll it out to my congregation and expect everyone to grow in the same way and at the same pace. It would be easier to manage and easier to measure. But I'm not sure that's the most effective way to make disciples, and it's certainly not the best way to create true community.

We should be in the business of serving God's purposes and not our own. Discipleship should be the result of a relational process, not a manufacturing process. Instead of building a system and asking leaders to serve that system, at NCC we reverse the formula. We teach people that we're called to make disciples, and we encourage them to get a vision from God for how they are uniquely designed to do that. Then we equip them, empower them and unleash them to run with that vision. We want our leaders to be motivated to make disciples where their passion meets need.

We have only two basic requirements for NCC small groups. I like to call them the bumpers in the gutters. If you're a really bad bowler or if you take small children with you to the bowling alley, the manager puts bumpers in the gutters to ensure that you and your party hit some pins. We put two bumpers in the gutters of our small group ministry to make sure our leaders knock down some pins: the relational bumper and the transformational bumper.

For a gathering of people to be considered a small group at NCC, they must be relational. In other words, one of their purposes for gathering must be to create an environment in which people can connect with one another and with God. This one's pretty intuitive and easy, and it's probably inherent in any small group gathering. The second bumper is transformational. We want every group to be in the business of making disciples in some way. That is, one of the purposes for gathering should be to help people take one step closer to looking like Christ and living like him.

We want to encourage innovation and creativity, because we believe that God has designed each person uniquely, and he can use that uniqueness as a catalyst for disciple making.

## Successful Experiments

We've experienced a lot of amazing experiments at NCC: the semester system; From Garden to City; Leadership Retreat. We'll talk about some of these experiments in subsequent chapters. But most of our experiments revolve around the kinds of groups we have. Here are some examples.

*Living Room.* One of my favorite examples of experimental community is the Living Room, a small group that meets every Wednesday in the basement of our church coffeehouse, Ebenezers. Every time I walk into the Living Room, I'm struck by the diversity. It's almost unsettling. Young, ambitious Capitol Hill staffers in suits sit next to sixty-year-old, unshaven war vets who call the streets their home. Bright-eyed twenty-somethings from the evangelical bubble of suburban America listen to a single mom who lost contact with her kids and eventually lost her home several years ago.

As they sit around a common table, sharing food and encouraging one another in their faith, I can't help but think I must be getting a glimpse through a window into heaven. The group started about five years ago as a ministry to the homeless community around Union Station. Each week, a team of volunteers would cook a meal, invite the homeless guys in and go through a Bible study with them.

Now, that would be a great story if we just left it right there. But it gets better.

Many of the folks who joined that leadership team did so because they saw it as a way to give, invest and serve. Over time, however, they discovered that they weren't the only ones giving. They were receiving from their homeless friends, who had fascinating insights into Scripture and a desire to help set up tables and chairs and serve meals. It wasn't just a service project for middle-class, evangelical twenty-somethings anymore. It was a community that was growing together.

*Fantasy baseball.* Several years ago, Nathan Gonzales asked if he could start a small group around a shared interest in fantasy baseball. To make it a legitimate "discipleship experience," Nathan sought to make it both relational and transformational. They would play fantasy baseball, and they would adopt a Little League field in the neighborhood. Every Saturday during league play, that group of guys would go to the field early in the morning to cut the grass, chalk the lines and prepare the field for games. They did it every weekend for several seasons.

Over time, people started to pay attention. Relationships formed. The small group hosted an All-Star Game party in the basement of Ebenezers. A National Community Church banner was hung in left field. Nathan was asked to throw out a season-opening pitch. People began to ask, "Why are you doing this?"

Guys—some of whom weren't involved in a regular small group and may have had no interest in getting involved in one that focused on how to serve the community or how to share your faith—found themselves doing all of the above. They were learning to share their faith, not because they had a workbook with blanks to complete, but because people were asking them questions about why they were doing what they were doing.

> **Some of NCC's interest groups excel at discipleship. The fantasy baseball group Heather talks about is a great example. But sometimes that transformational bumper in the gutter gets a bit deflated. I don't know that I can put an exact percentage on it, but we've certainly had our share of nontraditional groups that don't ever get beyond being relational to being transformational. Of course, we've had Bible studies with the same problem. But that's a whole other issue.**
>
> *WILL JOHNSTON*

Instead of cracking open a book that would make them think their way into right ways of acting, they were acting their way into right ways of thinking. I honestly don't think every small group must have a "study" component to connect the participants to God. Most of our groups do have a book or study element, but the fantasy baseball group is an example of how people can be discipled by "going and doing" with a leader who brings biblical and Christ-following intentionality to activity. Discipleship isn't about completing a workbook or doing inductive study of a book of Scripture; it's about reproducing the character, ways and mission of Jesus in others and expecting them to reproduce it in others as well.

*Artist group.* Mary Evans is a very talented musician. Amanda Giobbi is a crazy dancer. Dennis Bourne is a choir director. They decided to create a small group for artists, and they decided to bless the community by offering free arts classes to underprivileged kids in DC who didn't have access to that kind of training. From there, the whole idea began to snowball into a vision that was, in my faith-filled opinion, too big for them to pull off. This small group created small group environments for kids to learn dances, music, acting and graphic design, and then put all those skills to work on developing a show.

The adult leaders were insane enough to believe that impossible things could happen. They convinced the Atlas Theatre, a new performance theater on H Street, to host the kids' show, and they persuaded the bars on H Street to sponsor the event and offer prizes for a benefit raffle. In August 2009, a group of kids who had never had access to professional training found themselves on the stage of a legitimate theater, performing to an audience of raving fans, family members, friends and people from National Community Church.

But they weren't just performing; they were doing a benefit concert that raised money that went back into the community to provide arts training for kids. That would be an amazing end to the story, but it didn't end there. Several of the girls who were involved in the performance began attending our church.

Here's what I love about all of these experiments. They emerged from the heart and the passion of a leader. None of those ideas were mine, and I would never have come up with the ideas on my own. I'm thankful that my job as discipleship pastor at NCC is not to dream up all the ideas about how to create community and make disciples. My job is to unleash the imaginations of our leaders by helping them discover their gifts, passions and interests, and then leverage those for making disciples. My job is simply to encourage, equip, empower and unleash. If my job were to generate all the great ideas, we'd have a pretty anemic discipleship program at NCC. And that's all it would be—a program. Instead we have relationships that are on mission.

Those are just a few of the experiments that have been successful in the lab of discipleship at NCC, but we've had a number of flops too. We've had to admit some mistakes, discover some flaws in the system and recognize that some of our best ideas ceased to be good ideas. When we step into the world of the experimental, we learn plenty about failure. Sometimes it ends with a quick flush down the drain; other times we have to call in the hazmat team.

## Experiments That Failed

My first experience with small group ministry many years ago was an experiment in failure. For three years, I dreamed of being a small group leader. The church I attended had a strict process for stepping into leadership, so it was a long waiting period before I was selected and trained. When I was finally given the green light, I immediately recruited a coleader and began to prepare myself mentally and spiritually for the new challenge. I trained, prayed and even fasted.

Then I invited friends at church and friends at the biological engineering department to my small group. I even made some cold calls on people who filled out connection cards at church the previous weekend. I had no idea who was going to come, but I burned with a holy conviction that the Holy Spirit was going to show up and that this was going to be a small group to remember.

The night of the first small group gathering arrived. I rushed home after classes, cleaned the house, set out the snacks, reviewed the lesson and prayed once more. My coleader, Daniel, arrived. We prayed together. And we waited for those lucky souls who were about to find their life changed in the presence of God as they were ushered into it with my awe-inspiring leadership and curriculum facilitation skills.

Huh. It's already seven o'clock. Well, students run late, right? 7:13. I wondered if the address was right on the listing. 7:28. No one is coming tonight. No problem. God probably wanted us to have one more night to prepare ourselves. After all, he is about to blow our minds with what he's going to do.

Fast-forward one week. More invites. More phone calls. More snacks. A little more prayer. 7:00. Well, at least Daniel is here. 7:08. Really? Why can't students be a bit more responsible and get here on time? 7:17. Oh, okay, no one is coming. 7:33.

For the first two months, no one showed up to my first small group.

Experiments can fail on a number of levels and for a number of different reasons. Maybe the idea was just bad in the first place. Like the time I decided we should stop publishing all the small group listings in our small group magazine since people could just find them online anyway. Every time we launched new groups, we published a magazine listing of our small groups with leader contact information, details on the date and time, and a brief summary of the study topic and expectations. By the time we had grown to fifty groups, the publication of this magazine was becoming unwieldy.

As I thought about sustainability, I made a unilateral decision to move all our group information online and use the magazine only to promote a small number of "core discipleship" groups and to tell stories of life change. I reasoned that we needed to be more sustainable; people were more likely to look for a group online; it was easier to look for a group online; and our congregation would respect our environmental integrity.

I was wrong. I underestimated three very important things. First, the members of our congregation actually liked having a hard copy of the listings. Second, individual leaders were using the magazine as a recruiting tool for potential members. Under the old system, they could meet guests, invite them to their small group, hand them a magazine and circle their group and contact information. Third, and perhaps most important, I had underestimated the value our leaders placed on seeing their group listed in the magazine. There was a level of credibility and affirmation that came with the listing. One year later, we added group listings back to the magazine.

Was this a fatal error? Not really. But we certainly suffered in group recruitment and leader morale.

Maybe there's a good idea that isn't communicated or executed well. Like our A18: Neighborhoods. A few years ago, we decided to experiment with our first "alignment series" or "all church small groups series." We wanted all our small groups to follow a sermon-based curriculum for six weeks. Now, I knew this went a little bit against our free-market philosophy, but I felt we had developed a curriculum that allowed plenty of flexibility for people to keep gathering in free-market ways and put the study into practice in free-market ways. In my excitement about rolling out our summer strategy, I broke one of the first rules of leading change: I didn't communicate to our core volunteer leaders and earn their buy-in. I thought it would be a lot more fun to build momentum for it at our annual leadership retreat and do a big unveiling there.

Fail.

It had taken me about six months to develop this idea in my mind and a few more months to massage the strategy with staff and my highest level of volunteer leaders. Why did I think there would be automatic buy-in with the rest of the leaders the first time I mentioned it in a fifteen-minute infomercial at a leadership retreat? Well, it seemed like a good idea at the time.

But the failure didn't stop there. The implementation could have used some improvement as well. Since we were asking all small group leaders to follow the same curriculum for the first time, you'd think I would've developed the curriculum as soon as possible and ensured it was in the hands of our leaders early. Nope. And when our fantastic writing team put the curriculum in my hands, I did a poor editorial job of giving the materials consistency and a singular voice.

Overall, the experiment could be categorized as a "win." We launched more groups than ever before, new leaders stepped into leadership, and the impact on our communities was measurable. Even the feedback we received from our very honest and direct leaders was positive overall. But there were certainly parts we could have done better, and there were lots of lessons we learned for next time. Failures processed well lead to a better experiment the next time.

Maybe the cost-benefit structure of your system has contributed to a failure. We have a low bar for leadership. In general, this works great for us. But sometimes we wind up with real goons in group leadership. Like the time we approved a guy to lead a small group only to later discover that he listed his religion as "Buddhist Christian" on his Facebook site. We were able to catch that and put the brakes on his leadership before the group started, but our structure made it easy for that to slip through.

Maybe there's a well-executed flop. Like the time we tried to help our leaders develop an understanding and appreciation of the book of Leviticus by dressing up one of our team members in a rabbi costume to lead Levitical Challenges games. Yeah, that one resulted in us offending quite a few people—including some folks on our staff.

Sometimes our systems are thrown to the mercy of simple human errors that escalate into great problems. Like the time I developed a spiritual growth assessment for our leaders to use with their groups. The idea was to answer a series of questions about spiritual practices and beliefs and then go over the results with a leader or another trusted group member. Because of the sensitive nature of some of the questions, I included a statement in the guidelines to remind participants that the review should happen in a gender-specific environment. The guideline read, "Women should meet with women and men should meet with me." Oops. *Men.* Not me. *Men.* Dang spell-checker.

Or maybe we've created a great product, but no one is interested in it. We church people excel in that particular failure. A cereal company once asked its engineers to figure out a way to improve the production process of one of its most popular cereals. They were using technology that had been in place since the 1920s, which required a five-story building and a huge steam boiler along with many other monstrous, loud pieces of equipment that regularly broke down.

The process engineers were able to replace all this equipment with a device that would fit on a tabletop. It would cut capital and operating expenses by a substantial margin and required very little maintenance. The other advantage was that the old equipment produced a very inconsistent product. Some pieces of cereal were misshapen, some were broken, and some had odd holes that would cause the sugar coating to glob on the surface. All of these inconsistencies were random, but the new process produced perfectly consistent cereal pieces with no irregularities and no random oddball pieces. The engineers had wildly succeeded. The equipment was smaller, cheaper, more efficient and produced a better product.

However, when the replacement cereal was tested on the public, it failed miserably. The public hated it because it didn't seem like the old cereal they were used to, so the cereal company abandoned the new design and retained the old technology.

Moral of the story? We can create a perfect system that doesn't make a difference. We can implement perfect systems and perfect processes, but if no one wants them, they're no good. Perfect systems can be perfect failures.

I think the most important thing to remember is that failures are important to the process. A few years ago, I toured an exhibit at the Smithsonian dedicated to Jim Henson, creator of *The Muppets* and *Sesame Street*. While we know him for his successes, I was even more impressed by his many failures. Henson never stopped learning, never stopped growing and never stopped trying new things. Whether it was the creation of puppets that were never brought to life, the development of story ideas that never moved past the script, or hundreds of drawings that never found expression, he never let failure slow him down. It seemed that failure was a step to success.

## Experiments with a Shelf Life

We love experiments that succeed, and we learn from experiments that fail. The third category includes experiments that were once successful but have come to the end of their usefulness. In the church world, we need to remember that the message is sacred and eternal but the methods are temporal. We are often guilty of giving excessive life support to experiments that have simply come to the end of their shelf life.

Because of the transient environment of DC and the entrepreneurial culture of NCC, we cycle through experiments quickly and are constantly killing experiments that served us well at one point but are no longer producing the best results.

One example for us was a blog site called ZoneGathering. We launched ZoneGathering in 2005 to provide updates, resources and training to our small group leaders. In 2009, we killed it. And we probably should have killed it a year before that. It had simply outlived its shelf life.

More recently we have systematically replaced old small-group support structures and systems that were no longer adding best value for our leaders. It was a process called Operation Kaboom, and we'll talk about it more in chapter seven.

## From Classroom to Laboratory

Most of us run our small groups like a classroom. We aren't necessarily lecturing from the front, but our groups tend to focus on content, and our goals revolve around completion of a curriculum. There's a tendency for us to fall into the trap of replacing spiritual workouts with spiritual workbooks. Discipleship is not about having the right answer to write into a blank. It's about allowing our relationship with Christ to change us and the way we relate to others. Why not move your group paradigm from the classroom environment to the lab? Here are just a few ideas for experimenting in your group.

*Shake up the current components.* Change the way you engage your Bible study or the way you pray. Maybe it's changing the snacks. Forgo the traditional chips and salsa one night and encourage everyone to bring a food or snack that represents their childhood or the place they are from (watch out if you have a lot of internationals in your group—those flavors and aromas don't always mix well). Bring ingredients to make pizzas. Change up the flow of your meeting by moving prayer to the front end. Share leadership by asking each person in the group to facilitate discussion one night.

*Serve together.* There's learning that happens face-to-face, and there's learning that happens shoulder-to-shoulder. Face-to-face learning happens as we sit around a table and share our thoughts, opinions and feelings. Shoulder-to-shoulder learning happens when we go on mission together. Find a way to move your group out into the community on mission together, because when you serve together, you grow together. You grow closer in your relationship to one another, and you grow spiritually.

Instead of praying for your community together, why not send your entire group out into the streets and onto the sidewalks to pray on-site, asking a simple question, "How might you want to use us to bless this neighborhood?" Then come back together, talk about the experience, share any impressions you might have received through prayer, and then do it. Meet with your mayor or city council or school board to see if there's a practical way your group can bless the community.

> **This seems to be a good time to mention that Heather is famous for saying, "You attract who you are." Not surprisingly, I was once called the Apprentice of Goon when traveling with her to one of her speaking engagements.**
>
> **MAEGAN HAWLEY**

*Play together.* You can often learn more about people by playing with them for a couple of hours than by talking with them for a couple of hours. When Ryan and I go to New York City, we always stop by Colony Music to pick up some new karaoke CDs. After one trip during which we dropped an absurd and slightly embarrassing amount of cash on them, Ryan said, "Think of all the community it will build." He was right.

We all understand and acknowledge the importance of prayer in our small groups (even if we don't always practice it well). But I don't know that we have a good grasp on the theology of fun. As silly as it sounds, a little karaoke, volleyball, cornhole, tennis, softball, spades, Settlers of Catan, kayaking, Ping-Pong or soccer might be the most spiritual thing you can do sometimes.

Experience together. Shared experiences cement relationships, and if the experiences introduce some pressure or friction, they can help us grow. Find a worship gathering that's very different from your own tradition, and go to it as a group. I've taken my small groups to Franciscan monasteries, Greek Orthodox churches, Stations of the Cross services and Anglican churches. I've introduced them to icons, saints, Pentecostal gifts and Reformed theology. Watch a movie and discuss the spiritual themes. Find ways to put into practice the things you are learning.

## So, Go Ahead and Experiment

There are ways of making disciples that you have never imagined. Validate community where it exists, embrace an experimental posture, and dare to believe that God has wired each person to make disciples in a way that's unique.

What are your gifts? What are your interests? What are your hobbies? Where are your current spheres of influence? How might God want to leverage those to create community and make disciples?

When you experiment, you can count on making and cleaning up some messes, but that's the only way to make new discoveries.

# Lead Yourself Well

*If you want people to follow you, give them something worth following.*

**JIM WIDEMAN**

Follow my example, as I follow the example of Christ" (1 Cor 11:1). That's the kind of statement that gets the apostle Paul slapped with labels like "arrogant" and "egotistical." Follow me. Imitate me. Do what I do. I'll follow Christ and you copy me.

There was a time when those statements drove me crazy. Why didn't Paul just take himself out of the equation and tell people to follow Christ? Why did he establish himself as the great object of emulation for his disciples instead of Christ himself?

Paul knew something that I am only just now beginning to recognize: we all need a role model, a picture of Christ that makes the heart, mind and ways of Christ visible and tangible. To step into a role of leadership is essentially to state, Follow me as I follow Christ. We may never issue that challenge verbally, but that's the inherent call of leadership. Follow me. If people are going to follow us, our primary task is to lead ourselves well and endeavor to become leaders worth following. It doesn't take strong leadership when things are going well and everyone is getting along. But when you step into a place like Corinth, as Paul did—where people are fighting over lifestyle, doctrine and wine at Communion—leadership requires character and skill. And that takes work.

In Romans, Paul exhorts those who have a leadership gift to steward it well. We can't just hope to become a good leader or just pray to become a good leader; we must work hard to become leaders worth imitating. We have to bleed, sweat and spit our way through the mess.

## Follow Well

The first step toward leading yourself well is following well. There are literally thousands of books on leadership. I recently searched Amazon.com and found that there were twenty thousand book titles containing the word *leader*. Where are the books on *following*? Here is the reality: we all follow somebody. And if you are a Christ-follower, the practice of following well is fundamental to your identity.

I believe that the ability to follow well is one of the greatest tests of our character. The ability to follow a person you don't like or don't respect is a sign of maturity.

In 1 Samuel 16, David was anointed the next king of Israel, and "from that day on the Spirit of the LORD came powerfully upon David" (v. 13). In the very next chapter, David found himself in the palace, serving King Saul. Day after day, he worked in the palace serving the man in the position to which he was called. And the man he served was a terrible boss. Saul made poor choices, was not respectable and was known for trying to kill his employees. He was so bad that he barely knew the people who worked for him.

Saul first employed David to be his personal musician. He loved David's music so much he decided to make him his armor bearer too. After David's big showdown with the giant Philistine, Goliath, Saul asked the commander of the army whose son David was and where he was from. Evidently he had never expressed much personal interest in his court musician and armor bearer. Not long after that, he launched a campaign to kill David. That's not exactly the kind of boss you're going to throw a party for on Boss Appreciation Day. But David served.

If we keep reading the story, we find that Saul hunted David, yet David refused to harm him, even when presented with the opportunity. Not just once, but twice. David was a better person than I am. If I were ever offered an opportunity to kill the person who was trying to kill me, I'm pretty sure I would knock him out. Maybe I would have recognized it as a "test" of my loyalty, humility and work ethic. But the second time around, I'm pretty sure I would convince myself that God was giving me a sign that it was time to get rid of the guy and step into my calling. Not David. He followed well. And he mourned that he'd even cut off a corner of Saul's robe. Real leaders never feel the need to promote themselves.

Let's review. David had already been anointed king and had assembled an army awaiting his commands. Saul was not a godly man, and David could have easily convinced himself of the importance of killing him. It would be good for the nation, good for morale, good for self-defense and what a holy God would want. Those are easy rationalizations. Instead he rooted himself in the knowledge that God had appointed Saul their leader for that season for a reason. And David was convinced that God would get him on the throne if he would support Saul's administration.

Our generation needs to rediscover a respect for authority.

I'm absolutely convinced that God will get you to where he wants you to go if you give yourself to helping others get to where they need to go. I believe that God will give you an opportunity to chase your vision if you have proven yourself in being faithful to another person's vision. If you submit to the authority of God, you position yourself for God to grant you authority. We need to follow well.

I'm also convinced that God will not allow us to step into our giftedness and calling fully until we have first served another. He won't give us people to help us accomplish our vision until we have first worked to accomplish the vision of another. It may mean serving a leader we don't like or respect, but if we truly believe in the faithfulness and sovereignty of God, we can trust that he will get us where we're supposed to go when we're supposed to get there.

Who are you following? A pastor, a small group director, a ministry leader, a boss? What is difficult about following that person? How can you follow better?

## Friend Well

"Your friends will determine the quality and direction of your life."[1] I heard Andy Stanley say that in a sermon once, and I have repeated it often. You don't become you in a vacuum. The people you surround yourself with mold you and shape you into the person you were created to become. As you develop as a leader, think about the people who are rubbing off on you.

Let's go back to David for some inspiration. Here are a few of his friends:

*Jonathan.* One of the most unexpected stories of the Bible is the unlikely forging of the famous friendship between David and Jonathan. Since many of us heard the story as children, and it was infused with a healthy dose of saccharine fluffiness, we often fail to grasp just how astonishing and noteworthy that friendship was for both of them.

Jonathan was Saul's son. A brilliant and intrepid warrior in his own right, he was the rightful and anticipated heir to the throne. (Read about his audacious attack on the Philistines in 1 Samuel 14.)

David was the youngest son of a large family and looked after the sheep in the backwoods of Bethlehem. Nonetheless, the prophet Samuel declared and anointed him the next king of Israel.

After David slaughtered Goliath, Jonathan initiated the friendship. Defining the relationship meant that Jonathan gave David his robe, tunic, sword, bow and belt. That's a lot of loot. Jonathan became friends with the man who should have been his enemy and the biggest threat to the throne, and David trusted that friendship.

This is the kind of friendship that comes along only once or twice in anyone's life—if at all. Jonathan sacrificed for David. He literally gave him the coat off his back, was willing to go the extra mile for his friend, and spoke highly of David and sought to protect him even when it meant risking his own reputation or even his own life (1 Sam 19:4).

What strikes me as most interesting about their relationship is that Jonathan's rightful place of leadership and David's prophesied place of leadership apparently never entered into their friendship. It was never an issue. We need friendships like that. Friendships that carry with them no demands or expectations and are based purely on who we are, not on the title or position we have. We need friends who love us for who we are. Friends who don't let callings or talents interfere with the friendship.

I'm incredibly thankful for a small group of women I call the Hungry Mothers. On the surface, it's a bit of a misnomer. Only

one of us is a mother, but we're all actually always hungry. We
named ourselves after the location of our first retreat: Hungry
Mother State Park. These girls were friends with me before I
ever got the crazy idea to go on staff as a pastor at NCC, and the
way they related to me didn't change one bit after I did. I'm
grateful for them because I can strip off every hat of authority
and every role that I play and just be Heather with them.

Everybody needs a Jonathan—someone who recognizes the
gifts and callings but doesn't allow that to be the stumbling
block in the friendship. Someone who helps you get to exactly
where you need to go, even if it's not convenient.

Who is that person in your life? More importantly who are
you being a Jonathan to?

*Mighty men.* We also need some friends who are on mission
with us. Fast-forward a few years. Saul hunted David. In the
process, David lost his job, his wife, his home and easy access
to his best friend. Let's go straight to the pages of Scripture to
get a picture of what happened next: "David left Gath and escaped to the cave of Adullam. When his brothers and his father's household heard about it, they went down to him there.
All those who were in distress or in debt or discontented
gathered around him, and he became their commander. About
four hundred men were with him" (1 Sam 22:1-2).

Men in trouble, in debt or just plain discontented. What a
mess. David's life had bottomed out, and the last thing he
needed was a bunch of misfits bringing their baggage and bad
attitudes to the cave with him. But these four hundred men
were the people God placed in his life during that time, and
David embraced them. Before long, this bunch of raggle-taggle
misfits emerged as David's army.

Sometimes the best friends show up in the most unlikely
places in the most unlikely packages. One chapter later, we

read that David's army had increased to six hundred men (1 Sam 23:13).

A few years later, the army had grown and matured into a powerful and elite fighting squadron known as David's mighty men. We don't know how many of these mighty men came from the original ranks of the troubled, indebted and discontented, but undoubtedly at least some of them did. These brave warriors risked their lives for David before he became king of Israel, and they remained loyal to him throughout his reign.

Their names are listed and some of their stories are told in 2 Samuel 23:8-29 and 1 Chronicles 11:10-47. For example, Benaiah chased a lion into a pit on a snowy day and killed it. Jashobeam killed eight hundred men in one battle. Eleazer stood by David's side when the rest of the army fled, and Scripture tells us that he killed Philistines in a barley field until he could no longer lift his sword. Abishai killed three hundred enemies with a spear in one battle.

David's mighty men were on mission with him. There's no way he would have succeeded without those guys. And you won't do everything God has called you to without friends who are on mission with you. You may have moments when you're in the cave of Adullam, but at some point you've got to leave the cave and go out to do the things you are called to do.

We need people who understand and embrace what God has called us to and are willing to jump in and invest *their* lives in the work that God is doing in *our* lives.

My mighty men are found within a circle I call Team D. This is my term of endearment for the group of talented (not misfit) leaders I get to work with on discipleship at NCC. They are on mission with me and on mission with one another. Will and Maegan are not just coworkers or colleagues. They are in the trenches with me.

Think about the people whose voices are loudest in your life. Does God's purpose for your life seem bigger or smaller when you're around them? Does *God* seem bigger or smaller when you're around them? Mighty men call us to great tasks and encourage us to pursue God's heart. Make sure you have some in your life.

**Nathan.** David also had a friend who knew when to kick his butt back on track when he strayed from the path of good leadership. That guy's name was Nathan.

You probably already know the story. David was at the wrong place at the wrong time, committed adultery and then orchestrated murder to cover the sin (the whole ordeal can be found in 2 Samuel 11). He was fifty years old and had stopped being on mission. Instead of being on the battlefield with his mighty men, he stayed behind at the palace and got into trouble. When the prophet Nathan confronted David, he didn't just storm into the palace and start ranting and calling down judgment. He took the artistic king aside and began to tell him a story of injustice. The story sparked righteous indignation within the king, thereby allowing the rebuke of the prophet to worm its way into his heart through the back door.

We need people who will confront us, challenge us and give us a good swift kick in the butt. Dietrich Bonhoeffer said, "Nothing can be more cruel than the leniency which abandons others to their sin. Nothing can be more compassionate than the severe reprimand which calls another Christian in one's community back from the path of sin."[2]

Nathan didn't care that David was king and didn't worry about what David could do to him. And that's a good thing, because David's leadership would have been totally derailed without Nathan.

We need friends who recognize we're people in need of encouragement, correction and rebuke and who will gently but directly point us back toward God and his path. We need friends who love us but love God more and know that we can be better. Good Nathans don't just point out mistakes; they also identify what's already good and seek to strengthen what has the potential to be better.

A Nathan can arrive from an unexpected place and in an unexpected package. A package like Jenilee LeFors. This intern (we call them protégés) served as a Nathan in my life a few summers ago when she sent me an uncharacteristically pointed e-mail asking me for a completion and submission date for a book proposal I had been dragging my feet on. This perpetually bubbly and cheerful person typically saturated her e-mails with smiley faces, exclamations points and hearts. Not this e-mail. Black text on a white background with a direct and clear message: do it and report back to me. Later she talked to me about it in person. Again, no smiles, and no love except the tough kind.

Yeah, I needed to finish that proposal. But I didn't need an intern to be my accountability. The nerve. The audacity. Doesn't she know I'm the one who's supposed to enforce deadlines and kick butts? To be honest, I'm very thankful for that audacity, because that simple e-mail led to the words you're reading today.

We often call this kind of friendship an accountability relationship. Who has permission to ask you any question at any time? To whom do you confess your sins? Who is praying for you and confronting you when necessary?

*Samuel.* We need Jonathans who are loyal friends and unimpressed that we carry a title. We need mighty men who are committed to being on mission with us. We need Nathans who will speak uncomfortable truth into our lives.

And we all need a Samuel.

Let's roll the tape all the way back to 1 Samuel 16. Saul failed to lead himself well, rendering him a leader unworthy of following, and God directed Samuel to anoint a new king for Israel. Jesse paraded all his boys in front of Samuel. Except David. He was the youngest and had responsibility for the family's sheep, so even his father didn't think he was a worthy candidate. But Samuel didn't see a shepherd boy. He saw a king—not because of his appearance or abilities or credentials, but because he heard from God.

We need Samuels. People who have supernatural x-ray vision into our lives and see potential, gifts and callings in us that no one else sees. People who see what only God can see and speak those things prophetically into our lives. Who are we being these Samuels to? Who is doing this for us?

My lead pastor, Mark Batterson, is a prophet of potential. While most people looked at me and saw an environmental engineer or a political policy advisor, Mark saw a discipleship pastor. Mark sees things in people that no one else sees. He also sees potential in people that they don't see themselves, and he patiently calls it out of them.

Your friends will influence the quality and direction of your life. And you can do the same for others. Where are people taking you? Where are you taking people?

## Cultivate Character

Becoming a leader worth following also means developing the character you need to sustain the leadership you have been called to. We often invest a lot of mental energy and prayers into determining God's will for our lives: where he wants us to live, what he wants us to do and who he wants us to do it with. I'm convinced that God is much more concerned about who we're becoming than where we live, what we do or who we're with. Those dynamics certainly influence the person we grow into. But ultimately he is more interested in our character than in the task we're doing.

I would argue that character competencies are more important than leadership skills. Communication, decision making, vision casting and strategic thinking can often be learned and developed. Integrity, humility, responsibility, trustworthiness and reliability must be cultivated. They must be forged behind the scenes, in the thankless jobs and in the vortex of unfairness.

We can learn a lot from the character of Daniel. The Babylonians had invaded Judah and whisked many of its people into exile, but a few young men with great potential were hand selected to participate in a program that would prepare them to assume positions of political influence. Daniel was among them. He found himself in the court of a king whom he should treated as an enemy. But over the course of three foreign administrations, Daniel served well. His story shows that character sustains calling.

From Daniel's life, we learn that character is built through transformation, not information. We can't educate our way into good character. It comes in the crucible of tension, conflict and hardship. Daniel found himself in some sticky situations. Messes. Those messes shaped his character, and his character sustained him through the messes.

Pre-decisions are the most important decisions we ever make. They are the decisions we make ahead of time that provide guardrails and make game-time decisions easier and more resolute. In the opening chapter of Daniel, he and the other boys in the training program were granted daily portions of the best food in the kingdom. There were a couple of problems with the food, however. First, it wasn't kosher. Second, it had been sacrificed to Babylonian idols. Daniel could have complained to God about the terrible situation he was in. He could have chosen to eat the food, believing it to be a worthy compromise. He could have felt sorry for himself and mourned the loss of his Jewish identity and culture. After all, if he just followed the rules, perhaps one day he would be in a position to change them.

Or he could rely on a pre-decision that he had made. In verse eight, we read that he "resolved not to defile himself" (Dan 1:8). What have you resolved to do? What have you resolved *not* to do? The answers to those questions will chart the course of your life and leadership.

Solid pre-decisions include things like deciding ahead of time that you don't have a price. Deciding ahead of time that what God thinks of you is more important than what people think of you. Deciding that offending the Holy Spirit is far worse than offending people.

**Heather has a price. It's fried pickles and Corky's Barbecue.**

*WILL JOHNSTON*

Character is also built by being faithful in the small things. The nineteenth-century preacher Phillip Brooks said, "Character is made in the small moments of our lives."[3] Some might say it's wise to choose your battles, but you can't choose your battles when it involves your integrity. When it comes to character, every battle is important and there's no room for compromise. Our character is built one decision at a time. When Daniel was a young man, he made a difficult pre-decision not to touch food that would be dishonoring to God. That decision had the potential to affect his career. Several years later, Daniel would confront another decision that had the potential to cost him even more—his life. Had he not built his integrity in the small decisions of faithfulness early on, he might not have had the fortitude to face the lions' den.

Here are some questions to help us think through our character:

- How well do I treat people who can't do anything for me?
- Am I the same person in the spotlight, around friends and alone?
- Do I quickly and voluntarily admit when I've made mistakes and take responsibility for them?
- Do I have an uncompromising moral compass for decisions, or do I allow circumstances to determine my choices?
- When I have something to say about people, do I talk to them or about them?

## Run the Bleachers

Murphy High School. Bleachers. Running. Up and down. Over and over again. For an hour minimum. Day in. Day out. What would lead a generally normal and smart high-school student to engage in such a stupid and seemingly pointless ritual?

Track team. Four-hundred-meter run.

I hated running bleachers. But in every sport I played, we were forced to participate in stupid drills. Infield drills. Running drills. Sliding drills. Dribbling drills. Footwork drills. Volley drills. While I just wanted to get out on the court or field or track and do my thing, my coaches kept forcing me to do stupid, pointless exercises. I figured they did it because they didn't know how else to fill up the practice time. Or they just thought it would be a fun way to keep us busy. I would have been more than happy just to play the game.

As I matured, I realized I couldn't play the game without the drills. They weren't pointless. They were designed to make us stronger, quicker and more intuitive. They made us people of instinct. Drills prepared us for the game.

I think spiritual disciplines are the same way. Exercises like prayer, fasting, confession, worship and journaling can become dry and rote, and sometimes I start to wonder if God commanded us to do them just to keep us off the streets. Now that we're Christ-followers, he has to give us something to do to keep us busy, right?

To be honest, I sometimes find them pointless. Surely you've experienced it too. Ten minutes into prayer and that nasty inner voice questions the sanity and productivity of what you're doing. Now, when I encounter the tense, painful and important moments in the game of life, I realize that spiritual disciplines, like athletic drills, aren't meant just to keep us busy. They prepare us to play to the best of our ability. They train us into Christlikeness. The disciplines and the drills aren't the goals; rather, they are the preparation to attaining the ultimate goal.

Paul wrote to Timothy, "Have nothing to do with godless myths and old wives' tales; rather, train yourself to be godly. For physical training is of some value, but godliness has value for all things, holding promise for both the present life and the life to come" (1 Tim 4:7-8). Becoming a leader worth following requires training, and that means implementing some spiritual drills.

First, set some goals. Just as we can't drift into good character, we can't drift into spiritual growth. I've found that I never hit a goal that I don't set. So I examine my spiritual disciplines and try to set SMART goals for them: Specific, Measurable, Achievable, Require faith and Time-related. A SMART goal for me isn't "I'm going to read my Bible more." It's "for the month of January, I'm going to read through the book of James once a week and write down daily observations that I can practically apply in my life."

Second, I change my routine. If you always work out the

same way, your muscles grow accustomed to the routine and are no longer affected by it. The same is true with our spiritual workouts. If my Bible reading becomes boring, I pick up a new translation. Once I've read a verse or a passage too many times in the same translation, I begin to read right over it without allowing its meaning to penetrate my heart. The Bible has a very high shock value on most pages, but I miss it when I think I already know what it says. All of us do that because we read with a tainted perspective, which scientists refer to as heuristic bias—an accustomed way of thinking about something. Reading from a different translation can make those familiar passages come alive and shock me out of my spiritual lethargy.

Occasionally I change how I pray and what I'm praying for to break out of old, predictable, stale cycles. If I've been praying a lot in solitude, I try engaging in more community prayer. If I've been saturated by community, I seek solitude and silence. Sometimes I explore spiritual disciplines outside my own tradition like the Ignatian Examen or Stations of the Cross. We need to change our routines so they don't become routine.

Finally, I journal. I know a lot of people who are thankful that the words "and Jesus rose early and went out to journal" don't appear in the Bible. To be fair, it's difficult to build a case for journaling using a biblical proof text, though it could be argued that the entire Bible is a sort of journal. I've found that journaling is a good discipline for me. When I journal about what God is doing in my life, I see more of God in it.

It's sort of like my days in biology lab when the professor required me to observe organisms under the microscope and then draw them in my notebook. I hated it. It was embarrassing. Had I wanted to draw things, I would have taken an art class. But when exam time rolled around and I was forced to identify different types of microorganisms, I learned the lesson: you see more when you have to observe it closely enough to draw it. I think the same holds true with journaling. When I reflect on what I'm learning or experiencing and write it down, I learn more and I see more.

Set goals. Change the routine. Track your progress. Run the bleachers.

## Develop Tough Skin and a Soft Heart

A few years ago Mark, my boss, friend, mentor and pastor, gave me some important leadership advice: you've got to develop thick skin and keep a soft heart. That was helpful to me as a biological engineer stepping into a ministry role that some thought I wasn't properly prepared for. It's also helpful advice when I'm criticized publicly by people who don't know me privately. Thick skin and soft hearts keep us in the right posture and help us respond well.

I'm so grateful I'm called to leadership. I experience the presence and pleasure of Christ when I am leading, teaching and mobilizing teams toward a larger purpose. But sometimes leadership is lonely, and sometimes leaders become the punching bag for someone else's insecurities and issues. How we respond in the mess of those circumstances reveals our character and sets a course for our eventual success or failure. Developing tough skin while keeping a soft heart gives us the right posture and perspective.

Many of us default the opposite way. We have soft skin and hard hearts. We allow criticism—whether constructive and helpful or damaging and hurtful—to pierce our skin and leave wounds. Then we harden our hearts as a defense mechanism. That leaves us wounded on the outside and hard on the inside, rendering us unable to minister, lead or relate to others effectively.

Developing thick skin means we let the stupid stuff bounce off, not allowing an arrow to pierce our skin unless it first pierces through the truth of Scripture. Keeping a soft heart means remaining transparent, vulnerable, teachable and pliable in the hands of God and in our relationships with others.

I've found that there are four kinds of criticism. First, criticism that's correct in content and comes from a heart that's oriented toward Christ and our own growth. That kind of criticism should be welcomed—even craved.

Second, we get criticism that comes from a heart that's right, but the person got the facts wrong. In those instances, we should gently correct the misunderstood situation and aim primarily to honor and validate the relationship.

Third, the criticism is correct in content but comes from a heart that's not seeking what's best for us. This is the hardest criticism to navigate. In situations like that, we've got to distinguish between the kernel of truth and the clothing it's wrapped in. Prayerfully embrace what needs to change without being adversely impacted by a personal vendetta.

Fourth, some criticism is just incorrect and comes from a bad attitude. We usually find this in the form of e-mails and anonymous blog comments. That's when we hit the delete button and ignore it.

Just a few final thoughts:

- Don't let an arrow of criticism pierce your heart until it first passes through the filter of Scripture.

- If an arrow of criticism does pass through the filter of Scripture, let it pierce your heart deeply.

- Surround yourself with people who love you, are for you, have your best interests at heart and will tell you when you're being stupid.

- Ignore anonymous idiots whose criticism is invalid. And if someone you know gives you criticism that's invalid, don't waste time dwelling on the criticism. Focus instead on protecting the relationship.

- Express gratitude to those who have the courage to give criticism that's life giving and productive.

This is much easier said than done. But we've got to do it.

## Be a Learner

"Can you assign me a mentor?" This is a question, or a variation on a question, that I hear a lot. It always strikes me as odd, because I would never want to be assigned a mentor. I think a lot of us have heard people talk about the importance of having a mentor or speak glowingly of their mentor relationship, and we feel we'll never become the person we're supposed to be until we find one for ourselves.

There's a lot of information out there about how to be a good mentor—how to train, coach, lead, disciple and guide others into growth. But there's not much to be found on how to be mentored or on the characteristics of a good mentee. I would argue that learning to be a good follower is just as important as learning to be a good leader/mentor.

Here are some ideas for finding a mentor:

1. *Take initiative.* Be proactive in looking for projects and relationships that will be beneficial to you. Projects give you opportunities to invest your gifts. Relationships give you opportunities to develop and grow your gifts. Don't wait for people to teach you; take the initiative to learn from them. Take the initiative to find a mentor; don't wait for one to chase you down. I would avoid even using the word *mentor* in the beginning, because that tends to freak people out or

put lots of pressure on them. Just look around and pick out some people you would like to spend time with. Find some who have been around the sun a few more times than you or seem to have maturity in an area in which you'd like to grow, and ask them if you can spend a few minutes with them over coffee. If it seems to click with a particular person, ask if he or she would be willing to hang out again.

2. *Cross-pollinate.* There's a tendency for us to want to find that one all-knowing, all-wise guru—the grandmaster for our lives. My experience indicates that I find the best guidance within a community of mentors. I have mentors who help me with my writing and speaking, while others speak into personal areas of spiritual growth. Another camp speaks more directly to my relationships and marriage. Look for a team of coaches.

And while I'm talking about the importance of cross-pollination, let me give you some coaching to encourage cross-pollination. When people ask me how to develop their preaching gift, I tell them to take an acting class. Engineering taught me more about discipleship processes than a Bible class. Explore a diversity of interests, and look for the connection points and the metaphors between those disciplines and the leadership that God has called you to.

3. *Ask great questions.* Henri Nouwen said, "We have to keep looking for the spiritual questions if we want spiritual answers."[4] Always have a couple of questions ready to go. What have you accomplished that you are most proud of? Tell me your story. What character trait needs to be developed in my life? What three books have influenced your life and/or leadership the most? As you look at my generation, what is your greatest prayer for us? What is your greatest hope for us?

What one piece of advice do you wish someone had told you when you were my age?

4. *Take good notes.* Have you ever wondered why we have the books of 1 Timothy, 2 Timothy and Titus in our Bibles? Those were personal letters written to specific individuals. They weren't intended to be timeless doctrinal treatises, and yet they ended up in the canon of Scripture. Evidently those young pastors found the content valuable enough to keep and pass on. Benjamin Franklin (it's believed) once said that the shortest pencil was longer than the longest memory. It's important to capture what you're learning, so it's probably a good idea to carry a notebook and pen wherever you go.

5. *Set specific goals.* Once you enter into a more formal mentoring relationship, make a list of five things you would like to learn or experience with your mentor. I've had so many meetings and conversations with people who were convinced they wanted a mentor, but they had absolutely no idea what they wanted a mentor to do for them or teach them. Having goals is a starting point. It will help you find the right mentors for the right things and will bring definition, purpose, clarity and intentionality to the process. It's also a good idea to set a time limit on the formality of the relationship so you don't get into a rut where you are wasting one another's time.

6. *Add value.* When possible, add value to your mentors. Don't just ask mentors to take time out of their schedule to invest in you. Find ways to get involved in what they're already doing and contribute to their goals. If they're leading a ministry team, jump on it. If they're leading a missions trip, sign up. If they're painting their house, pull out your paintbrush. If they've got to run errands, offer to drive them. I'm con-

vinced that we learn better when we're in the trenches with folks rather than sitting across a table from them. You can learn by watching and add value to their life and leadership at the same time. Find ways to advance the dreams of your leaders, and it's likely they will reciprocate. Hint: if you see someone you'd really like to spend time with but you aren't sure you would ever be able to get on that person's schedule, use this approach to cause your schedules to collide.

It's also helpful to realize we can find mentors in the margins and from a distance. What if you made it a habit to try to learn something from every person you encountered? Ralph Waldo Emerson said, "I have never met a man who was not my superior in some particular."[5] In other words, each person we meet has the potential to teach us something. Make learning your passion, and look for the lesson in every situation. Approach every situation as an opportunity to learn.

Also, look for mentors from a distance. I've been mentored by folks I've never met because I've read their books, followed their blogs or listened to their podcasts. You can even be mentored by dead people. I count Augustine, John Wesley, John Calvin and Martin Luther among my mentors because they have left a written legacy behind.

## Examine Your Motivation

Let's be honest. Every now and then we just don't want to go to small group. Even though we're the leaders. *Especially because* we're the leaders. Maybe it's been a long day and we're tired. Maybe we just don't have the relational capacity to deal with the long talker, the weird talker and the person who lingers for an hour after everyone else leaves. There are nights when we just don't care about that prayer request for Aunt Beulah. Or we didn't have time to do our homework that week. If you haven't experienced this yet, you probably haven't been leading for more than a few months, or perhaps you are a much better person than I. What do you do when the last place you want to be is your own group? It's time for a motivation check.

There are many reasons we step into small group leadership. For some of us, it's a genuine love for people and a desire to see them grow. For others, it's an opportunity to invest their gifts. Some see a need and want to fill it. There are a few that simply cannot *not* lead. But at the end of the day, there's only one viable and valid reason for doing what we do: to see God's name honored and glorified in our generation.

Our love for people will fade every now and then. A situation will arise that causes us to question our giftedness, and a day will come when our passion wanes. The cost/benefits of meeting the need will not add up. We must do it for God and God alone.

You are going to encounter mess. If you want to become a leader worth following through the mess, you have to lead yourself well. You won't hit a target that you don't set, and you won't drift into spiritual maturity. You've got to be intentional and develop a plan. Follow well. Friend well. Cultivate your character. Discipline yourself spiritually. Learn from mentors. Grow tough skin and keep a soft heart. Be motivated by the right things. We need to grow so we can say to those who follow us, "Follow my example as I follow the example of Christ."

# Growing People

*Growing people grow people.*

**MAC LAKE**

The calendar had flipped to December, but we were clad in shorts and T-shirts. This was football in the raw. No pads either. We also weren't really tackling. The ball was at the ten-yard line, and the two teams pulled up to the line of scrimmage. One lineman was distracted by the bug he noticed crawling across the grass. The center snapped, I ran to the end zone, cut left and looked for Mike. He threw. I caught. Touchdown. Cheers, yells, hugs.

During the day, Mike Mathews served as the pastor of a local church in Texas. But on holidays, he turned into a neighborhood hero and semiprofessional athlete in Mobile, Alabama, where he assumed the role of all-time quarterback for kids' pickup games. What I loved about Mike was the way he made me great on the field. He always set me up for the great catch and the touchdown. It never really occurred to me that he was doing that for the other kids too; all I knew was that Mike believed in me and was willing to create environments for me to win. That built trust that turned into a relationship that I have turned to over and over again for advice, direction and counsel. Whenever I had questions about jobs, calling, gifts and pretty much anything I considered to be a major life decision, Mike was on the other end of the telephone or e-mail.

When I was in high school, Mike began to nurture my love for the Bible, leadership in the church and ministry. He introduced me to the concept of discipleship and talked about the potential for small groups to facilitate spiritual growth. He bought me books and recommended churches to learn from. I listened to everything the man said, because he earned my trust in the backyard of a home in Mobile.

Mike was a coach and a cheerleader all at the same time. He was also a champion for the story he saw God writing in my life and continued to encourage that. We all need coaches—those who believe in us and make investments in us. We need people who will grow us, and as we grow, we intuitively and inevitably grow others. Mac Lake said it best: "Growing people grow people." If you're growing spiritually, you'll grow people spiritually.

Growing people is more important than growing programs. Discipleship is dependent on relationship, so we've got to ensure that our leaders are involved in life-giving and growth-inspiring relationships. If our leaders are growing, our groups will grow and our discipleship strategies will grow. But such growth requires strategy and intention.

## Discipleship Vision

To grow people effectively, we've got to have a vision for discipleship. In 2 Timothy 2:2, Paul outlined a strategy for growing the church: "And the things you have heard me say in the presence of many witnesses entrust to reliable people who will also be qualified to teach others."

Those were among the last words Paul left to his disciples: what you heard me say, pass on to others who will pass it on to others. That was the plan. Really? That's the best strategy God could come up with? The Creator, Redeemer and Sustainer of the universe left the history of his kingdom to a game of worldwide telephone? (You remember that game, right? The one where you sit a dozen people in a circle, whisper a phrase in the ear of the first person, who whispers it to the next, and on and on it goes until the person at the end announces whatever ridiculous thing she or he heard that bears absolutely no resemblance to the original.) That just seems odd to me. Couldn't God come up with a foolproof plan? Maybe even one that would bring him back to earth for some visits from time to time? Hadn't the disciples already proven their inability to comprehend the message and keep the story straight?

Nope. That's the plan. The story of God must pass from generation to generation. People must become living, breathing vessels of the gospel of Christ and pour themselves into others. We are here today because those guys two thousand years ago dared to believe that discipleship works, and they passed the faith from one person to the next. It's now been left to us to pass the faith on to the next generation.

## Value People over Programs

What do you value most on the first night of small group? The number of people who show up? Or the one life that begins the process of change?

Leaders who leave a legacy see the value in individuals. They realize that ministry isn't a program; it's people who are moving in the overflow of their gifts. Disciples don't emerge from a program; they emerge from relationships. While I invest a great deal of time thinking through structures, strategies and programs that will facilitate life change, I'm convinced that ultimately discipleship must be carried out by some*one*, not some*thing*. It takes time, attention, energy and prayer.

Paul's ministry was one of relationships. Even the letters he wrote were relationally driven. He wasn't just putting books on shelves for anyone who might want to pick them up. He was writing very personal correspondence to specific people in specific places about specific situations. He was writing to friends, fellow ministers and people he was intentionally investing in.

One of my favorite parts of his writing is Romans 16. We often think of Paul as a task-oriented, no-empathy, rough kind of guy, but this chapter reveals his heart for people. As he closed his letter to the church in Rome, he listed about three dozen names of people who had served as his mentors, disciples, teammates and spiritual family. Priscilla and Aquila, Erastus, Phoebe, Rufus and Gaius were just a few.

Romans. The closest book we can find to a systematic theology in the Bible. Paul's statement of faith. It's not exactly the kind of text that would seem to lend itself well to commentary on subjective things like community, but as is evident in Romans 16, no personal statement of faith is created in a vacuum. It's a reflection of the voices that surround us. Paul ended Romans with a list of names—people who had shaped him and formed him, people who had invested in him, people who had taken a risk on him, people who had been crazy enough to join him. When I come to the end, who will be on my Romans 16 list? Who will be on yours?

Paul demonstrated how he valued Timothy when he referred to him as "my true son" and "my dear son" in the letters he wrote to him. He told Timothy to fan into flame the gift that he received when Paul laid his hands on him; so evidently Paul deposited some sort of spiritual gift into Timothy. He told

Timothy not to let others look down on him because he was young, but to be an example to them.

Paul recognized that it wasn't just his preaching and his writing that would carry on after him; his most important legacy was the investments he made in people. In fact, when we look at the qualifications that he gave for leadership in the church, most of them are directly related to how a person interacts with other people (1 Tim 3). It's not about gifts or leadership ability so much as it's about self-control, reputation, gentleness, integrity, faithfulness to a spouse, being respectable and managing a family well.

People who leave a legacy invest their time and their gifts in other people. Consider a story of two preachers: George Whitefield and John Wesley. In the 1700s, the spiritual climate of a generation was shaped by these two important figures. Both preached to huge crowds and led high-profile ministries, but their legacies look a little different.

Whitefield was regarded as the best preacher of his time, and he has left us a legacy of biblically rich and stirring, convicting sermons that are as relevant today as they were then. Wesley was a good preacher, too, but he valued investment in people over the perfection of a sermon. His legacy can be found in the millions of followers in churches all over the world who have been left in his wake.

I'm not knocking the ministry of Whitefield at all, because I believe both men acted according to the unique mission God gave them. Personally I'd rather be a Wesley than a Whitefield; I want to leave a legacy that's found not only on some dusty bookshelves but also in the everyday, walking-around lives of people. That's harder to do, because you can't see the immediate success.

Recognizing that his legacy was dependent not only on his

94COMMUNITY IS MESSY

own gifts and abilities, but also on the gifts and abilities of
those he discipled, Wesley organized his followers into groups
called "class meetings." At each meeting, the participants
shared what they were learning from Bible study, what they
were praying for, where they were struggling and where they
were growing.

Wesley also invested significant time and energy in the development of young preachers. Even today, you can visit the
chapel that he built at Bristol, in which he installed a glass window above the sanctuary from which he could watch his young, emerging ministers preach. Afterward, he would meet with each of them and discuss their progress.

More than two hundred years later, we see the powerful results of Wesley's choice to make people his priority. His movement brought us the United Methodist Church, the Methodist Church of Great Britain, the African Methodist Episcopal Church and the Wesleyan Church, representing millions of Christ-followers today.

**Little-known Team D fact: We don't have an accurate way to measure numerical growth in small groups. Beyond a few annual surveys of our congregation and the overall number of registered groups and leaders, the primary way we measure growth is by stories of life change. That is largely a reflection of Heather's leadership. While measurement serves good purposes and we gather data the best we can, Heather lives and leads out of the value of people over programs.**

*MAEGAN HAWLEY*

So, what should we value most? How many people show
up? How well we led a group discussion? We tend to value
most the things we can measure most readily and easily, but
making those things a priority might short-circuit the greater

purpose of a group. If we value the growth of one person—no matter how long it takes—we will build the kingdom of God through people.

Leading groups isn't so much about figuring out the logistics of your meeting schedule, preparing a lesson or making sure snacks are available. Invest time in conversations, in creating memorable experiences and in taking people on adventures.

## Employ X-Ray Vision

Sitting in freshman English class feverishly working on a paper, I glanced up to notice that Coach Henderson was at the door, talking to our eccentric guide through American literature, Mrs. Smith. Strangely their attention seemed to keep turning in my direction. Next thing I knew, I was being summoned. Evidently someone had shown the coach some of my times from P.E. class, and he wanted me on the track team.

The track team? Softball team, absolutely. Tennis team, most definitely. Volleyball team, sure. Track team? I would have never pictured myself on the high-school track team. But he made the big ask, and to everyone's shock, I ran in circles (and up and down bleachers) all spring instead of running around a diamond or a court.

Seven years ago, I was advising a U.S. senator on issues of environment and energy policy while wondering when I would get back into my boots and be out in the field, working as an engineer again. Most people in this city viewed me as a policy advisor. I viewed myself as an environmental engineer. Enter Pastor Mark. He saw something very different from what I or anyone else saw in me. He saw a discipleship pastor. And that has made all the difference in my life.

Will Johnston leads the charge for discovering and deploying new small group leaders at NCC. But just a few years ago, he was simply a participant in a men's group. In his own words, "When I was in Jonathan Shradar and Gary Officer's men's group, Jonathan asked me to help them lead it. I had led an Alpha group a year or two earlier but hadn't led anything since and just needed someone to ask."[1]

There are two common threads in these stories. First, leaders looked at followers and saw something no one else seemed to see. They had x-ray vision like the prophet Samuel had when he saw a king in the body of a shepherd boy. Second, they made a big ask.

I think you have to be a little crazy to be a disciple maker, because you have to see things in people that others don't see. You even have to see things in people that they don't see themselves. And then you have to speak things into their lives or ask them to do things that they may scoff at or at least shake their heads and laugh at.

When Samuel looked at David, he didn't see a little shepherd boy; he saw a king. Jesus looked at a big-mouthed fisherman and said, "You are Peter, and on this rock I will build my church" (Mt 16:18). When Barnabas saw Saul, he didn't see a murderer of Christians but a preacher and missionary. When Paul saw Timothy, he didn't see a young punk kid, and told him, "Don't let anyone look down on you because you are young, but set an example for the believers" (1 Tim 4:12).

In the previous chapter, we talked about the importance of having a Samuel. In this chapter, I'm pushing you to be a Samuel to someone else. If you need someone to believe in you, acknowledge your potential and give you opportunities to excel, start doing that for someone else.

Effective disciple makers have x-ray vision. They look beyond the external and have supernatural insight into another person's gifts, potential and calling. It's developed when we keep one ear to the Holy Spirit and one ear to people. Discernment is most definitely not one of my spiritual gifts, but I've found that the Holy Spirit gives me insight concerning the people he has entrusted to my care.

One of the greatest leadership lessons I've learned is to never say someone else's no for them. Sometimes it feels awkward or even embarrassing to make big asks. What if they say no? That's fair. They might. But what do you have to lose? The answer will also be no if you never ask. If you ask, there's a chance they will say yes.

Here are a few ways to ask:

- "I see potential in you, and I'd love to see you leading your own group in a year."

- "I need some help leading this group, and I think I would really enjoy getting to work more closely with you. Would you help?"

- "I've noticed that other people in the group seem to listen closely to you and respect your ideas. Have you noticed that? I think you would be a great small group leader."

Jonathan had to ask Will to lead, and now Will spearheads making the big ask for small group leaders all over our church. Pastor Mark had to ask me to come on staff—and kept asking for three years.

## Look to the Future

T-ball: I played second base and garnered more votes for the All-Star game than any other player on the team. Beginner softball: I played shortstop and hit in the lead-off position because of my consistent base-hitting percentage. Intermediate softball: I played third base because I had an impressive arm, and my team went to regional tournament play. My career had been good, and I was advancing into the high-school league.

On the first day of practice, my dad sent me to left field.

*Left* field? Left *field!* You're feeling the shock and horror, right? No? Okay, let me back up and explain some things.

Outfield is not where you wanted to be placed if you were playing ball at Mims Park. That's where the subpar athletes played. And when I say "athlete," I use that term generously. I'm talking about the kids who didn't care a lick about being on the team, the kids who were there because their parents made them, the kids who got distracted by the planes flying overhead or the worm that just popped its head out of the ground. Those kids were safe in the outfield because no one ever hit out there.

Infield was where the action was. Particularly the left side of the infield. I loved the speed, the thrill of the double play, the fast reflexes as the ball zipped down the baseline and the quick throw to first base. I couldn't wait to show off my skill in the high-school league.

Left field? Clearly my dad must hate me. He no longer believed in me. Obviously he must be trying to teach me a lesson; there could be no other explanation. Seeing the disdain on my face, he gave me a stern but reassuring look: "You will thank me one day. And that day will be soon."

Dad knew something I didn't know. In slow-pitch softball, high-school girls can hit, and they usually pulled it to the left side of the field. In one magical year, the entire game changed, and the new position of choice was left field. What Dad knew was that I would love left field more than third base, because left field was the place where all the action would happen. I couldn't see into the future, but Dad could. He had future vision. And that's another aspect of discipleship that's incredibly important—to see what lies beyond what most people see.

When we think of discipleship, most of us look primarily at the people sitting right in front of us from week to week. Those are the people we're called to disciple. But when Paul issued his charge to Timothy, he was thinking not just of his young protégé, but also of others much further down the line. He was thinking of those Timothy would disciple and those Timothy's disciples would disciple.

I love watching the ministry of Maegan Hawley. At only twenty-eight years, she's already living out this principle. Maegan led a girls' small group for a few semesters and then felt it was time to move on. So she passed the baton of leadership to Marion. As it turns out, Marion was even more popular than Maegan, so she had to split her group into several subgroups.

One night, I heard there was leftover Chick-fil-A at Maegan's house, so I decided I should probably swing by on my way home to help her get rid of it. When I arrived, her living room was packed with about a dozen girls from Marion's group who were being trained to lead their own groups. Maegan was not only investing in a Timothy, she was also investing in her Timothy's disciples.

The people we're leading today aren't just participants in our study. They're the people who will be leading people in the next study. They're the people who will be coaching the people who lead the studies. When we have a long vision like that, it changes the way we see people, interact with them and encourage them.

If you're a small group leader, implementing this principle means that you're aggressively raising up new leaders to do what you do. As Maegan says, "If you wait until your group is too big to raise up a new leader, that's not discipleship. It's damage control." Raising up new leaders isn't a solution to a problem—your group is too big, your group needs to split into multiple groups and so on. Raising up new leaders is the biblical challenge of discipleship.

## NCC Coaching Strategy

Like many churches, we've adopted a coaching strategy to support our small group leaders. Some coaching structures operate on the span-of-care principle (six to eight leaders per coach) while others are simply geographically based or homogenously arranged. In many of those systems, the best small-group leaders become coaches by default, regardless of whether or not that "promotes" them out of the position of their greatest giftedness.

At NCC, we've implemented a one-on-one coaching strategy that operates on the assumption that the best teacher is the best question asker. Coaches might be younger or older than the leaders they coach; they might be more or less experienced. What makes a good coach is a person who can listen, can ask good questions and can detect the fingerprints of God in another's life.

> **Our coaching strategy also operates on the reality that we have lots of young people and only a handful of older people, and that we have not really figured out how to best leverage the older people we do have. It would be nigh impossible to have all of our leaders be coached by someone who is significantly older and wiser.**
>
> *WILL JOHNSTON*

During new leaders' first semester of small group leadership, we assign them a coach. The stated goal is that they meet with that coach three times during their first semester to share their stories, talk about the importance of leading yourself well and explore concepts of building biblical community as it relates to their unique group situation. Reality check: most of our coaches are batting only .666 on this. Or even .333. I guess in baseball terms, that's still great, right? Three times is still the goal, but we aren't doing it perfectly yet.

After the first semester, a leader can opt in or out of coaching. We want every leader to be coached, but not every leader needs to be in relationship with one of our official, rubber-stamped coaches for the discipleship to be valid. Some of our leaders have great relationships with their campus pastors. Some of them have mentors from back home. Others find themselves sharpened by another leader they meet with regularly. We affirm that. If they're getting that kind of investment somewhere else, there's no reason to require them to reinvent it or try to manufacture it within our system.

Some leaders don't want to take the time to invest in their own leadership or don't think they need to. At some point, those leaders step into a mess and recognize the value of a coach. Or they quit. Either way, I was tired of watching my best coaches desperately trying to coach and care for people who had no desire to be coached or cared for. In our system, though prone to disaster, the leaders who want to grow the most are getting the most attention and the best investment from our coaches.

## NCC Training Environments

While our coaches care for the hearts of our leaders, our training environments focus on developing our leaders' skills. Here are a few of the ways that we do it:

- *Leadership 101.* Before people become small group leaders at NCC, they participate in an online training experience called Leadership 101. It's a combination of short teaching videos with interactive questions and essays designed to help new leaders think creatively, biblically and strategically about their group.

- *Leadership summits.* Once a semester, we gather all our leaders for a half-day of worship, teaching and vision casting. It's an opportunity for us to celebrate what God has been doing through our groups and ministries and to rally for the upcoming semester.

- *Leadership retreat.* Our annual leadership retreat is our largest leadership training event of the year. We take all our leaders offsite for twenty-four hours to pump them full of vision and training. It's a time when we go all out to honor and appreciate our leaders. It's an opportunity to cultivate and maintain our culture as a church. We are creative and believe in doing it right and doing it big, so we incorporate great music, produce great videos and even bring a little magic to the stage (seriously, one of our emcees is a magician who makes people disappear and stuff). We harness the event to remind everyone involved that leadership is simply being a disciple who makes disciples.

> Moving training online has been one of our biggest wins in recent years. Church trainings tend to be one-way. I—the expert—deliver content to you—the learner. But this doesn't give the expert much insight into the learners. Those same questions that help potential leaders think through how to lead give us insight into their readiness to lead.
>
> **WILL JOHNSTON**

## Travel Agents and Tour Guides

The goal is to disciple a life, not to teach a lesson. Edgar Guest said, "I'd rather see a sermon than hear one any day. I'd rather one would walk with me than merely tell the way."[2]

Some of the best discipleship advice I ever got was from a book on evangelism: it's more important to be a tour guide than a travel agent.[3] Travel agents sit behind a desk in the climate-controlled comfort of an office and give you brochures telling you where to go, how to get there, what to do once you're there and what you might see along the way. They may or may not have even been there before. Tour guides lace up the hiking books, strap on the pack and go on the journey with you. They've trekked the path before and can interpret the path for you along the way. Tour guides don't just warn you of possible dangers; they help you walk through them.

Good disciple makers are tour guides who see the hand of God at work in a person's life and point it out. Paul acknowledged the influence of Timothy's mother and grandmother in the development of his faith (2 Tim 1:5). He helped Timothy understand his spiritual history. Paul also used examples from everyday life—athletes, soldiers and farmers—to describe the work Timothy was called to do. People who leave legacies are able to make simple things profound and complex things simple. They identify the fingerprints of God in a person's life and help him or her understand how God is at work. They see the simple things in life and use them to paint pictures of our complex calling in God.

What does this mean practically? We can't just talk about prayer in our small groups; we've got to do it with people. We can't just complete a workbook on serving our community; we've got to get out there and serve. We can't just explain to people the best way to lead a group; we've got to do it alongside them.

Be a tour guide.

## Discipleship in the DMV

The best discipleship occurs within the context of real life. I coach a handful of leaders at NCC, and most of my coaching meetings happen over a great breakfast at my favorite restaurant

on Barracks Row—Ted's Bulletin. (If you're in DC, check it out.
And be sure to trade in the toast for a made-from-scratch
brown-sugar pop tart.)

In a moment of insanity, I once let one of my young leaders
convince me that the DC Department of Motor Vehicles was a
great place for a coaching meeting. At 7:00 a.m., when we were
about forty-five minutes into the wait in the freezing cold, I
realized this wasn't really about coaching but about being moral
support for running the arduous and intimidating gauntlet of
obtaining the elusive and coveted DC driver's license. We
covered a lot of ground that day, talking about her desire to
write, to find margin for more creativity and to figure out a new
approach to Bible study. She emerged from the DMV with some
spiritual goals and a new driver's license.

When I'm investing in others, I try to be intentional about
three things: conversations, experiences and celebrations.

*Conversations.* I try to focus my side of the conversation
more on questions than answers. The longer I try to be intentional about discipling, the more I realize that the best spiritual
leaders are not those who give the most right answers but those
who ask the most powerful questions. Jesus asked approxi-
mately 307 questions in Scripture. I've discovered you can go to
deeper places when you ask questions. Questions are memorable, stretching and penetrating. The right question at the
right time can make someone unzip her or his heart and crave
encouragement and correction. I always keep a handful in my
back pocket:

- Where do you see God most at work in your life?

- What is the biggest challenge you're facing right now?

- What fruit of the Spirit is most abundant in your life? The
  least?

- If you knew you could not fail, what would you attempt?

Good disciple makers have become skilled at the craft of constructing powerful questions and have cultivated the art of listening.

*Experience.* I also strive to capitalize on shared experience. For instance, I rarely travel alone. I know some people value the alone time they get on the road, in the plane and in the hotel. Maybe I will want that someday too. But for now, traveling with another person is almost a nonnegotiable for me, because it's an opportunity for that person to see who I am when I'm "on" and when I'm "off."

If you're going to the hospital to visit a group member, take someone along. If you're going to the bookstore to check out curriculum, take someone along. If you're going to meet with someone who mentors you, take someone along once in a while.

*Celebrate.* Mike Mathews was skilled at setting me up for a touchdown on the football field. He let me experience small wins that built confidence in my abilities and trust in his leadership. Good leaders do that. They set people up to experience victories and celebrate them when they happen.

I celebrate everything. When our aspiring writers blog consistently, I notice. When our artists confidently go to auditions, I applaud. When our young preachers deliver good sermons, I cheer. Celebrations could be dinners, a note or just a quick post on their Facebook wall. In most cases, consistency is more important than dollar value.

Let's make this practical. Who are the one, two or three people you could make more intentional investments in? And don't tell me there's no one with potential. That's just weak leadership. Remember, we have to *make* disciples, not *find* them. Got their names in mind? Write them down. Now, think

about a conversation you could have with each of them that
would help them take the next step forward in growth. Think
of a shared experience that could turn into a teachable moment,
and think of a way to set them up to experience a win and celebrate it.

# Discipleship Is Not Linear

*Never make a principle out of your experience; let God be as original with other people as He is with you.*

**OSWALD CHAMBERS**

The other day I was thinking about the modulus of elasticity. Yes, I tend to think about such things, and we can blame that on the six years I spent in engineering labs. The modulus of elasticity is the mathematical description of an object's or substance's tendency to be deformed elastically (that is, not permanently) when a force is applied to it. Once a material reaches the yield point, permanent transformation occurs. More simply, it's the point at which an object can be stretched and return to its original size. The more rigid the substance, the higher the modulus of elasticity.

For example, a rubber band has a very low modulus of elasticity. You can stretch it to double, triple and quadruple its size, but when the deforming force is released, the rubber band returns to its original size. Steel, on the other hand, has a higher modulus of elasticity. If you stretch it, twist it, compress it or deform it too much, its shape is permanently changed.

There's a parallel to spiritual growth here. So often, we implement disciplines and participate in experiences that stretch us, but they don't actually stretch us to our spiritual yield point. They don't take us to the point of permanent change. When we leave the retreat where we had a mountaintop experience, we swear we'll never be the same again. But by Thursday, our lives and our spiritual fervor have shrunk right back to the pre-retreat size and shape.

In the engineering world, you typically want to design so that the stresses on a material don't exceed the yield point. It's no good to have a bridge that breaks. But in the world of discipleship engineering, it's absolutely essential to stretch people past their yield points, which means we've got to recognize that one sermon or one class or one retreat won't produce permanent results. Implementing a new spiritual discipline for just a few days won't produce permanent change.

The modulus of elasticity also teaches us that discipleship can't be one-size-fits-all. Just as wood, steel and iron all differ in their modulus of elasticity and require a design that recognizes that, so each person in our congregation has his or her unique spiritual modulus of elasticity. We must design discipleship environments that offer flexibility and personalization.

For too long, we've assumed that God grows people in a one-size-fits-all, academic model of linear learning. But if we look closely at our own spiritual growth, we discover that we didn't learn to pray because it was the next stop on the church's discipleship path, but because we were thrown into a situation where everything depended on it.

I'd love to implement a one-size-fits-all discipleship strategy at NCC that's easy to manage, easy to communicate and easy to measure. But discipleship is not that clean. It's messy, and the spiritual modulus of elasticity is going to be different for different people. There will be different yield points and different environments that stretch and challenge different spiritual temperaments.

## The Path Has Strayed

In the second act of Stephen Sondheim's twisted fairy tale *Into the Woods*, Little Red Riding Hood cries out in a rare moment of desperate obedience, "Mother warned me never to stray from the path." The typically practical and compliant Baker replied, "The path has strayed from you."[1]

We try to keep people on the right path, which we usually write as a series of linear steps to spiritual maturity that we frame in academic terms, like Class 101, Class 201, and so on. We expend lots of energy and financial resources to keep people from straying from that path, because we're convinced the path is the key to their spiritual growth.

But perhaps the path has strayed from us. When our systems and structures and steps aren't working anymore, we have to take a big step back and reevaluate. We're finding that discipleship isn't linear. Or at least it's not linear in the way that I, the engineer, would like it to be linear. Or linear in the way that I, the one responsible for measuring the results of our small-group ministry, would like it to be.

Here are a few examples of people who have walked a path of discipleship that might seem to be off a more linear path:

Amanda came to the Neighborhoods and Nations small group because she wanted to be a part of a community that was socially conscious. That brought her to weekend services at NCC, which eventually led her to be cast in our production of *Steel Magnolias*. Now she serves on our staff team overseeing domestic missions.

When Sarah led Old Testament Survey, we expected the

group to fill up with kids who had been a part of NCC for a while and were looking for a meaty group experience where they could be "fed." Those folks showed up, but so did a Jewish girl with no relationship with Christ or any desire to have one. But the Old Testament provided her with some familiar ground to make some new friends and to hear about Jesus.

Sadaf was raised by Muslim parents but was not indoctrinated in the Muslim faith. He has never seen any religion as exerting an overall positive influence on history or culture because of the conflict that ensues over it, and he has never been interested in embracing it personally because it can't be empirically proven. Nevertheless, when Sadaf wanted to explore Christianity, he went on one of our missions trips. And not just any of our trips—the one that went right into one of the darkest corners of the globe, Uganda.

Katie joined our Israel missions team for a number of reasons—a boy, a political interest, a vacation from work. But she met God in the process. She claimed it wasn't so much the places she visited or the work they did that changed her but the people she traveled with. On the trip, she was baptized in the Jordan River, and she is preparing to move to Tel Aviv to get her master's in social work for trauma and crisis.

The path isn't as linear or as predictable as we've often assumed it to be.

## Dimensions of Discipleship

A few years ago, Pastor Mark and I talked about the need for a discipleship pathway. Because "everything is an experiment," we had developed some great discipleship and community environments, but we didn't have a clear process for people to grow in their faith more strategically and intentionally. The primary concern was for those who were just starting their faith journey and were asking "what next?" and for those who had been walking with Christ for a long time and were asking "what now?" We knew that our goal was to make disciples, but we needed to figure out how to get them from point A to point B.

While we kept using that word *disciple*, we wondered, "What does it even mean?" We tossed around a few definitions: A fully devoted follower of Christ. A learner. A person who does certain things and understands certain things. An apprentice. To provide any sort of pathway for growth, we first had to define the word. Is it about what they know or about what they do, or is it a description of who they are? Here is where we landed: A disciple is a "lifelong seeker of God and his ways, learner of his truth, influencer of culture and investor in his kingdom."

There are four dimensions of discipleship: seeking, learning, influencing and investing. We based this on the picture of community we discovered in the book of Acts. The story moves at a quick clip. In just the first two chapters, Jesus told his followers to go make other followers and then abruptly left. The Holy Spirit rained down on the believers in the Upper Room with tongues of fire. Peter preached his first sermon, and Jews from all over the Roman Empire heard the gospel in their own language. Three thousand people were baptized and added to the church in one day. In the midst of this action, the author hits the pause button, zooms out and gives us a glimpse of the day-to-day, real life of the everyday people who aligned themselves with this new movement. We see a snapshot in time:

> They devoted themselves to the apostles' teaching and to fellowship, to the breaking of bread and to prayer. Everyone was filled with awe at the many wonders and signs performed by the apostles. All the believers were together and had everything in common. They sold property and

possessions to give to anyone who had need. Every day they continued to meet together in the temple courts. They broke bread in their homes and ate together with glad and sincere hearts, praising God and enjoying the favor of all the people. And the Lord added to their number daily those who were being saved. (Acts 2:42-47)

Let's break this down to examine the characteristics and practices of those early Christ-followers.

*Learning.* The first thing we see is that the disciples devoted themselves to the apostles' teaching. There was an intellectual dimension to their faith that echoed Jesus' instruction that loving God is at least one-fourth mental as we love him with all our heart, soul, mind and strength. It's the process of transforming our character through the renewing of our mind, as Paul challenged the church at Rome (Rom 12:2).

Learning is the intellectual dimension of discipleship. This happens when we're actively reading, studying, memorizing and meditating on the Word of God, and it happens when we struggle to develop good doctrine and embrace the core beliefs of our faith. The way we think about our faith affects the way we live it out, and the way we think about God affects the way we worship. We want to make disciples who are able to worship God rightly because they know him.

*Influencing.* Next we see that the early band of believers was devoted to fellowship. They met together in the temple and in their homes, and they ate together. Discipleship was inherently relational in nature. It's what we would call being an *influencer.* They embraced the challenge of John 13:34-35: "A new command I give you: Love one another. As I have loved you, so you must love one another. By this everyone will know that you are my disciples, if you love one another." They were also influencing beyond the four walls of their houses. They enjoyed "the favor of all the people," and "the Lord added to their number daily those who were being saved" (Acts 2:47).

Granted, skip over a few chapters and we find that they quickly lost favor with some and suffered persecution, but the reality is that the first-century church couldn't be shoved to the margins of society. Nor did they seek refuge in carefully constructed cultural ghettos. They were either loved or hated, but they were never ignored. They influenced those around them by the way they lived.

Influencing is the relational dimension of discipleship. We want to produce disciples who share their faith with fellow believers and with those they meet in the everyday, walking-around places of their lives through evangelism. We want to influence neighborhoods and nations for the kingdom of God.

*Seeking.* The early believers were also devoted to prayer, and their prayers were so potent that they walked around in awe at the miracles that were following the apostles. Many of these people had seen the amazing feats of Jesus of Nazareth, and yet they were still amazed at what God was doing in their midst. We call that being a *seeker.*

Seeking is the spiritual dimension of discipleship. We want to produce disciples who practice spiritual disciplines, discover and implement their spiritual gifts, develop the fruit of the Spirit, understand and participate in the work of the Holy Spirit and engage in spiritual warfare. The word *seeker* has caused some confusion, because most people think of the word in the pre-Christian sense: "I'm hoping to invite my coworker to church because I think she is really seeking right now." We don't mean it in the sense of pre-Christian, beginner faith. We mean it in this sense of lifelong seeking after God. Since we're constantly forced to redefine the word for people, we're in the process of rethinking this language; but we'll address that in chapter seven.

*Investing.* Finally, we read that the disciples had everything in common. They sold stuff and gave the proceeds to people who needed it. They were *investors* in the kingdom. They knew what their assets were as Christ-followers, recognized that they were stewards and not owners, and leveraged their resources and time for maximum kingdom impact.

Investing is the stewardship dimension of discipleship. We want to produce disciples who are investing their finances, talents, time, energy and resources into kingdom work and whose calendars and checkbooks reflect kingdom priorities.

Seeking, learning, influencing and investing provide the framework for our discipleship strategies. We wanted to engineer environments in which people could develop as seekers of God and his ways, learners of his truth, influencers of culture and investors in his kingdom.

## Core Discipleship Groups

After defining our terms, we began to think through what we were already doing, could be doing or should be doing to help people grow into seekers, learners, influencers and investors.

As much as I love our fantasy baseball groups and running groups and moms groups, not everyone at NCC needs to be involved in those groups. However, we acknowledged that there were some groups that everyone could benefit from, such as the Alpha Course, New Testament Survey and Holy Spirit Encounter. We began to define those as our "core discipleship groups," and we finalized a list of groups, retreats and other experiences that we wanted to encourage NCCers to participate in during their time with us:

*Alpha.* We encourage all NCCers to begin their discipleship journey with Alpha. While we tend to be very entrepreneurial and don't like using prepackaged curriculum at NCC, we've implemented the Alpha Course wholesale and love it. Alpha is a twelve-week practical introduction to the Christian faith for seekers, cynics, skeptics and long-time followers of Christ. It begins with a big kickoff dinner and a video, *Is There More to Life?*

After the kickoff, participants are invited to come back for the full course, which includes weekly dinners, presentations on some aspect of Christianity (Who is Jesus? What about the Bible? What about other religions? and so on) and small group discussions. We've found that Alpha is a great first step for people, whether they're new to faith, new to NCC or revisiting their faith. We tell people, "Bring your questions, your doubts and your appetites."

Various denominations all over the world have implemented Alpha, which revolves around the idea of loving people into the kingdom of God. The hospitality and small group environment create a safe place for people to hear a dangerous message. (Get more information at www.alphausa.org.)

*Journey.* We decided we needed a "next step" after Alpha and a group experience that introduced NCCers to our vision for discipleship and the core discipleship opportunities. We created an eight-week curriculum called Journey, in which we introduced participants to the four dimensions of discipleship: seeking, learning, influencing and investing. Two weeks are dedicated to each dimension: prayer, sacraments, Bible reading and study, service, evangelism, community, discipleship, financial stewardship and spiritual gifts.

The other core discipleship experiences fell into the four categories of seeking, learning, influencing and investing. Most of them were traditional small group environments. Others, like being involved in a ministry or going on a missions trip, were not traditional small groups but nonetheless valuable to spiritual formation. While we never communicated that NCCers were expected to participate in these groups or should complete them before joining other groups, we did identify them as strategic growth opportunities that should be considered by people wanting to chart a course for personal discipleship and needing some guideposts for mapping their journeys. (See a list of those groups in appendix one.)

**We've got some great Core Discipleship groups. The trouble is that it has proven difficult to actually run all of them regularly. We're great with Alpha and financial stewardship groups. We do a decent job with our intro to theology group and our three-week overview of the Bible. But it has been quite a while since our last Old Testament group. We're just now starting to run New Testament groups again, and I'm not sure Neighborhoods and Nations has happened since the one Amanda attended years ago.**
*WILL JOHNSTON*

## Discipleship Map

Once we defined discipleship and identified all the groups, classes and opportunities that we thought every NCCers should experience during their time with us and categorized them according to relevant discipleship dimension, we had to string them together to create a process that made sense. We needed to systemize it, and that's where things started to fall apart and get messy.

Theology gets messy when we try to systemize it, as I've learned from leading our Theology 101 class over the past several years. Theology is supposed to create a path for us to see God more clearly, love him more deeply and live more like him, but sometimes we find that we can't quite reconcile all those questions about free will and God's sovereignty or the way sanctification actually works out in our lives. Our attempts at constructing neat, direct paths between one doctrine and the next often leave us running in circles. Those circles can either lead us to a place of awe and worship or send us into a tailspin that becomes more focused on construction of the path itself than on relationship with the Person.

The same can happen when we try to systemize the process of discipleship. Like theology, discipleship should help us learn more about God so that we love him more and live more like him, but sometimes our systems for accomplishing it become more focused on us and what we're doing than on God and what he is doing. We move the point of discipleship from relationship to a list of boxes to check off and find ourselves running in circles.

I didn't want a one-size-fits-all approach. The principle of the modulus of elasticity had convinced me that we couldn't just shove people through a gauntlet of biblical instruction and expect them to all emerge from that process the same. Some people grow best in one-on-one discipleship mentor relationships. Others grow best in community with a larger group. Meanwhile, a worship experience or a missions trip or a service project or a retreat may be a more powerful discipleship experience for some people.

I like academic lecture/lab discipleship. Give me a textbook and an assignment, and I start growing—it's not just an intellectual activity, it's discipleship for me. For most people, however, the academic environment isn't the best for discipleship, so I wanted to develop a strategy prayerfully that was built on a variety of discipleship methods and that was easily customizable for individuals.

Another issue we had to tackle was the "order" or "progression" in which we encouraged people to engage the core discipleship opportunities. The engineer in me likes to think in linear teams, but the artist in me recognizes that the spiritual growth process is different for each person. I'm also convinced that the process is often more important that the end product. As I tried to lay out our own version of a baseball diamond or metro-themed map or pathway to spiritual growth, I kept getting held up trying to figure out what came first—learning to study Scripture or learning to love our neighbor; learning to pray or learning to share our faith.

In my experience, there did seem to be a predictability and linearity to spiritual growth. For instance, I made a decision to follow Christ. Then I learned to practice basic spiritual disciplines and began to read my Bible. Once skilled in those, I started to share my faith with others. In high school, I just wore T-shirts with novel and often ridiculous statements reflecting spiritual themes and folk theology on them. I thought this would prompt deep and meaningful conversations about faith, but I think they primarily prompted or just confirmed the notion that I was a weirdo. But I digress. Once skilled at spiritual disciplines, armed with biblical knowledge and eloquent in selling the solution to the sin problem, I was prepared to embark on the ultimate expression of contemporary Christian martyrdom—the missions trip. That just seemed to be the path.

But the path seemed to stray from me when I started listening to the unique stories of emerging generations. Their paths looked very different from mine *and* from one another. I was reminded of Oswald Chambers's admonition, "Never make a principle out of your experience; let God be as original with other people as He is with you."[2]

In his poem "A Course on Creative Writing," William Stafford wrote of people who "want a wilderness with a map." I think that describes a lot of us. There's a yearning for the mystery, excitement and adventure of stepping into the unknown. But that yearning for adventure is held in tension by a strong desire for a map to show us where to go. There's something in us that wants to see the destination. While the unknown is exciting, it's also unsettling.

So at NCC, we decided to make a discipleship map. We took the concepts of seeking, learning, influencing and investing and turned them into islands that housed the groups, classes and experiences that related to them.

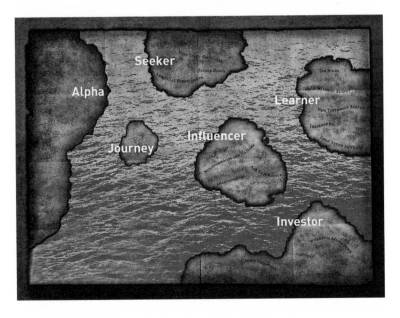

We encourage people to start with Alpha and then move on to the Journey island. From there, participants can determine in which dimension of discipleship they most want to grow. Each island contains a Port City, the group we would recommend for starting (Seeking—Spiritual Experiments; Learning—The Story; Influencing—Neighborhoods and Nations; Investing—Portfolio). While we have a recommended path for those who want it, we don't prescribe anything. If you want to start with Theology 101 (and some do), then start with Theology 101.

This map doesn't have all the answers. It doesn't include everything we need to do or learn to be a disciple, but it does give NCCers a general idea of some ways they can take the next step in their spiritual journeys.

We don't want to give people boxes to check off. Rather, we want to expose them to experiences that ignite their passion for God—and then get out of their way. The goal isn't to finish a process but to grow closer to Christ, so our aim is to give people opportunities to become fully devoted followers of Christ.

With the map, there's also terra incognita— places of growth we haven't yet discovered that require more experimentation and exploration. This leads me to the next confession and the subject of chapter seven: we're in the process of blowing this all up. We're rethinking our whole paradigm for discipleship and redrawing our map. The two principles we will hold on to are the ones we've just addressed: a customized approach to discipleship that isn't linear.

The point isn't to encourage you to copy these groups or use this map. The point is to recognize that discipleship is often not a clean, straightforward, linear process but a messy adventure. Look for the opportunities in your environment that everyone should experience, and find a way to put them on the map for people who are thinking through their spiritual growth path.

## Intersectional Discipleship

We tend to think that innovation is found in the slow evolution of linear developments around a particular idea. In the book *The Medici Effect*, author Frans Johansson introduces the idea of "intersectional innovation"—creativity that emerges at the intersection of two seemingly disparate ideas, concepts or fields of study. During the Renaissance, artists, scientists, poets and philosophers converged, breaking down barriers between disciplines and cultures, and ushering in one of the most explosive eras of creativity and invention. More recently, architects have designed energy-saving office complexes by studying termite mounds. Engineers have collaborated with biologists to understand the toughness of the conch shell and apply the principles to tank armor and automobile bodies. These kinds of innovators are reimagining life at the intersection of ideas.

Jesus was the master of intersectional innovation. He combined law and grace to give us redemption and salvation. He brought together Jews and Samaritans to paint a picture of community in his kingdom. And he fused humanity and divinity to give us the incarnation—a God who walked in our shoes and was tempted in every way and yet remained sinless and held the authority to save us from sin. He reimagined grace for the prostitute, reimagined righteousness for the Pharisee and reimagined life for the sick.

What happens when we allow ourselves to reimagine church at the intersection of ideas? Movie theaters and coffeehouses transform into places of worship. Martial arts meet compassion when a small group smashes boards to raise money for a homeless shelter. Faith and doubt collide on Monday nights to create a safe place to hear a dangerous message and ask difficult questions. We discover intersectional discipleship.

We work closely with our teaching team and creative team because there are times when a sermon series needs to penetrate our congregation more deeply than it can in thirty minutes on a Sunday morning. When the discipleship team collides with the teaching team, we discover all kinds of new ideas. Like A18 Neighborhoods, where we essentially turned all our small groups into short-term domestic missions teams for the summer. Or LXVI: From Garden to City, in which we read through the Bible as a church, blogged through the Bible as leaders, preached through the Bible on the weekends and studied through the Bible in small groups from Lent 2010 to Lent 2011. Intersectional discipleship produced The God Anthology, a nine-week sermon series on the attributes of God that was accompanied by small group curriculum developed by the discipleship team and an album of original music by our worship team. When discipleship pastors help worship leaders write music, all kinds of fun erupts. Once we got past the hilarious differences between the nerds and the hipsters, we found that our collaboration produced music that was more theological and Bible studies that were more worshipful.

We are also aware that a few moments can be catalysts for discipleship. We are looking for ways to better leverage moments like baptism, weddings and baby dedications to help people grow.

We embrace the idea of intersectional discipleship in our discipleship map. While everything is offered within the fabric of group life and within the semester context, not everything is a traditional small group per se. We want to work closely with our missions department because we recognize that going on a missions trip may be one of the most formational experiences a person can have. The preparation before a trip and the reflection after a trip can help us create some environments for intentional growth. We recognize that being involved in a ministry is part of spiritual formation, so we want to promote our weekend ministry opportunities as ways to find community and grow as disciples. We don't view the other programs of the church as competition but as additional opportunities for people to grow.

What do you find at the intersection of ideas in your life? It might be a new idea for a small group or a ministry or a missions trip. What happens when your skills collide with the heart of God? What happens when your greatest passion meets the world's deepest need? What happens when the eternal Word of God intersects our daily lives? Think outside the box. Reimagine community, mission, ministry and discipleship.

## Nonlinear Groups

Small group leaders can implement these principles for their individual small groups. Think about the topics you typically focus on in your small group. We all have dimensions of discipleship that we're partial to. For me, it's the learning dimension. I love Bible study and theology. One day I'm going to lead a parallel study on Leviticus and Hebrews, and people are going to love it. For my friend Pat Cooper, it's the seeking dimension; she loves to practice spiritual disciplines and loves to help people discover the joy and intimacy in Christ that can be found in solitude and silence. Josh Stockstill loves to create opportunities for connection and community and knows that growth will happen if the right people link arms to experience their faith journeys together. He is an influencer. These preferences tend to show up in the kinds of groups that we lead, so we have to be intentional about incorporating the other dimensions as well.

When I lead a learner-oriented group, I try to incorporate elements of the influencing dimension into our experience. The relational side of discipleship is driven by food, and I've found that serving dinner before Theology 101 makes the debate on Calvinism/Arminianism and Foreknowledge/Open

Theism more palatable. Furthermore, when we take a few moments to talk about how the debate changes the way we worship God and affects the way we treat others, it makes the study of theology more practical.

## This Ain't FedEx

Once upon a time, someone stumbled upon my blog because he had done a Google search on "how to shorten the discipleship process." How do I find the quickest means to the end? As though we could put the raw materials of humanity into a mechanized system and spit out perfectly formed disciples on the other end. Discipleship is about a completed workout, not a completed worksheet. It's about a journey, not a destination. It's about something we're always *becoming* (present tense), not something we *became* (past tense). It's about being in the process, not having arrived at the product.

I promptly wrote a new post to inform that person he should quit his job. This ain't FedEx; it's discipleship.

As leaders, we need to be aware of the ways the people in our group are growing and how our leadership is affecting that. Ultimately it's the role of the Holy Spirit to bring change in a person's life, but often we lead in such a way that we expect disciples to simply materialize if they're physically present in our groups. But Jesus told us to *make* disciples, not *find* them, which requires the investment of time and tremendous effort. All that blood, sweat and spit stuff.

If the people in our groups aren't growing, maybe we need to reconsider the way we're leading. If we get discouraged after one month or one year or even three, we haven't yet grasped that discipleship takes time. Twelve Galilean guys spent three focused years with Jesus himself and still didn't show up for the prayer meeting on the most important night in history.

When I think about discipleship process, I think about relationships and journey. Two steps forward and one step back. Conversations, experiences and moments shape us, but we don't see it at the time.

It's tough to be a small group pastor in a church culture that loves the event. It's easy to get excited about the outcomes of events: we have instant success, instant data, instant results. However, while events might spark change in a person's life, they rarely exceed spiritual yield points. Permanent life change happens much more slowly and imperceptibly, and it requires us to be committed for the long haul. If you think making disciples happens within the context of a once-a-week small group over one semester, you're crazy.

Change happens slowly. Gradual, consistent change over time is the best kind and the most lasting. A few days ago, I received an unexpected call from one of my mentors, Dave Buehring, who said something that really stuck with me: "Discipleship can't happen in sound bites." What a profound sound bite! He said it in a very casual, throwaway kinda way, but I think it's a statement of critical importance. In an age of short attention spans, meals in microwaveable boxes and life moments reduced to 140 characters, we need to recapture the ideas of longevity and endurance.

Discipleship is a whole life journey, not an eight-week class. It's about developing the fruit of the Spirit and spiritual gifts and looking more like Christ, not about checking off a set of boxes. It's a process of becoming, not a destination. There's no way to short-circuit discipleship. It's about turning every moment of every day into an encounter with God.

Read Paul's final encouragement to Timothy: "Fully carry out the ministry God has given to you. As for me, my life has already been poured out as an offering to God. The time of my death is near. I have fought a good fight, I have finished the race, and I have remained faithful" (2 Tim 4:5-7 NLT). These aren't the words of a man who had just finished a set of sprints. They are the words of a man who was on the last leg of a super marathon.

Consider some of his words more closely. He was "poured out as a drink offering" to God. Are we allowing God to pour us out? Have our lives spilled out all over those that God has entrusted to us? He "fought the good fight." If you want to shorten a fight, there are three ways you can do it: die, surrender or win. The final victory isn't something we can control, and I know I don't want to surrender. So I have to keep fighting until the death. Paul "remained faithful." Discipleship isn't about us and our schedules. It's about remaining faithful to God and to the people he has put in our path.

If someone discovers a biblical way to shorten the discipleship process, I'm all for it. Until then, I'm going to have to find some way to follow Paul's example. Remember, it's more about the process than the product. Growth isn't necessarily linear. And the best growth often happens at the intersection of ideas. If you sign up for making disciples, you've got to be committed to the long-haul, nonlinear mess of people's lives.

# Small Groups Should Happen in Real Life

*Life is about rhythm. We vibrate, our hearts are pumping blood, we're a rhythm machine, that's what we are.*

**MICKEY HART**

One of my favorite movie scenes is in the beginning of *Dead Poets Society*. The new English teacher at the prestigious Welton Academy began his first lecture as expected—by asking his students to read Dr. J. Evans Pritchard's introduction to their poetry textbook. But then he gave the students their first glimpse at his unorthodox teaching style. He told them to rip it out. He claimed it was complete nonsense. The introduction outlined a mathematical formula that made poetry an object of logic as opposed to an object of appreciation and wonder, and Dr. Keating believed it had no place in their textbooks. He wanted them to feel poetry, not dissect it.

I've often imagined myself in a similar scenario: standing before church leaders, pastors, volunteers and small-group hosts and exhorting them to rip page thirty-six out of their dictionaries. The *baht* to *balloon* page. It's thrilling to watch all those pages fly in the air in my mind's eye. We need to rip out that page to excise the word *balance* from our vocabularies. Contrary to what we've been taught, I would argue that balance has no place in the life of a leader. The problem with that whole page-ripping scenario is that we would also lose terms like *bake sale*, *balderdash* and *ball of fire*, and that would be tragic. But I just like to imagine the scene.

I've lost count of the times I've been encouraged to find balance. I've even encouraged others to achieve a life in balance. We've invested ridiculous amounts of mental, emotional and physical energy on trying to find balance. I decided a couple years ago to stop trying to strike a balance and to pursue life in rhythm instead.

Jesus doesn't look like a balanced man to me. On the day he received the news that his friend and cousin John the Baptist had been beheaded, he started off for the wilderness to be alone and pray. But then he saw the needs all around him and decided to teach and heal some folks instead. A well-meaning counselor would have been concerned that he was clearly in the denial stage of grief.

On the other hand, there was the time that Jesus slept through a near-death experience while crossing the Sea of Galilee. The waters were so deadly that even the fishermen were scared the ship was going to sink. Jesus is the kind of guy who gets distracted from healing Jairus's daughter by a random woman who touches his robe (Lk 8:40-48) He's the kind of guy who lets a woman off the hook for adultery but gives the religious people hell for asking a few questions. He talks of patience and then makes a whip and goes ballistic on the merchants in the temple. This is not the description of a balanced person.

But his life did move in a calculated rhythm. He withdrew to the wilderness to pray. He left the crowds to invest in the few. If we follow this man, balance will not be the outcome, but we can strike a sustainable rhythm.

## Unique Rhythms

For several years, my otherwise reserved and conservative mother has been convinced she would make an excellent drummer. While she has played the ukulele and the harmonica, she has had no drumming experience to my knowledge. When I asked her why she thought she would make a good drummer, she responded, "Oh, I have good rhythm."

One year, I found some air drumsticks in a kitschy novelty store. You just bang out your cadence in the air; no hard surface necessary. Mom found them in a box addressed to her under the tree on Christmas morning. We all sat around with great anticipation as she waved them confidently in the air. She could have been playing for Smashing Pumpkins. Or the Jamaican National Steel Drum Band. Or Lawrence Welk. We weren't sure. But it was fun watching her discover her rhythm.

Though I speak of NCC's semester system primarily from a descriptive perspective rather than a prescriptive perspective, I do believe that every church exists in a community that flows to a particular rhythm. I'm not an evangelist for the semester system, but I'm a huge proponent of finding your unique rhythm and allowing it to fuel your discipleship and community efforts. Jesus called us to live counterculturally, but I'm willing to wager a guess that his objective had more to do with our character and how we treat our enemies than whether or not we insist all our small-groups meet during the height of the T-ball championship season.

Life moves to a rhythm. And every church finds itself in the middle of a unique community rhythm. The rhythm in DC will be different from the rhythm in Nashville or Seattle or Opp, Alabama, or wherever you are. When you allow your small groups and discipleship programs to ride the wave of life, it creates momentum, gives balance to participants and ensures that group life becomes an organic part of real life and not a programmed add-on. Everyone has a unique rhythm that must be discovered.

## Semester System

Our small groups operate on a semester system. It's actually a trimester system, for those who want to be very specific about it. To be even more specific, we run our spring semester from February to the end of April and our summer semester in June and July, and we conclude the year with the fall semester from September to December.

When our lead pastor introduced this crazy idea to me, I thought it was the worst small group idea I'd ever heard. All the experts said that true community doesn't start to develop until about week twelve of small group life. There were even nice charts and graphs and timelines to inform me what stage of relational development and interaction might be normative for my group at week forty-seven. There were flowcharts to convince me that if we were still together by week 183, it was past time to multiply. And my own experience had shown me that by week forty-seven, we were sometimes still struggling to remember that redheaded kid's name and we would never be able to multiply unless some normal people found their way into the group. So wait, why did we even try this particular experiment?

No, I was not a fan of the semester system. Neither were several of my best leaders. We tried it only because we were still in the day when I thought I was merely a "placeholder" leader stewarding a system that would soon be taken over by another leader. My primary job was to lead well and implement Pastor Mark's vision and not to be the mouthpiece of common sense and conventional wisdom.

Why did we keep the experiment? Because it didn't take me long to realize that I would never go back. And many of the late adopters declared publicly that they would never go back either. (Is anyone seeing a theme of how often I have strong opinions and how often I have to reverse them?)

Here are some of the reasons we have adopted a semester system at NCC:

*Rhythm.* I know that Jesus commanded us to live counter-culturally, but I'm not sure that meant we must all meet with our small groups during the month of August. There's a natural rhythm in NCC, and we've decided to work with that instead of against it. Since so many people in our congregation work on the Hill or are college students, there are natural "break points" in the year for us. May, August and the Christmas holidays are always slow times. So following a semester system is natural for our culture. If small groups are for every real life, the rhythm of group life should match the rhythm of real life.

*On-ramps and exit signs.* I love visiting Newfoundland, but I hate driving there. The signage is terrible, and the maps aren't oriented north-south. At least not the one I was using. I missed many exits and failed to get on interstates where I was supposed to. I can still feel the frustration. (But, for real, you should visit Newfoundland. Make sure to go kayaking in Bay Bulls.) The point is, people are more willing to jump in and try a group if there are easy and obvious on-ramps and exit signs.

Most people don't want to merge into a preexisting group at an awkward time. Typically they like to be new when other people are new. The start of a semester is a great time to do that.

People also like exit signs. We've found that most prospective small group members are more inclined to try out a group if there's a clear exit point in the foreseeable future. If they find their small group exists somewhere in the tunnel toward awkward, they want to be able to see the light at the end of it. It's hard to check out a group if you suspect you'll be forced to pray with the same people at seven every Tuesday morning for the rest of your earthly life. When there's an obvious on-ramp and the commitment lasts for eight to twelve weeks, it's an easier step for people to take.

*Targeted discipleship.* Let's say you join a small group that's studying Romans together. And they study every word of Romans, every nuance of every word in Romans and every theological perspective on every word in Romans. That's going to take you at least a year or two. And let's say that about three months into that study, someone in the group recognizes there's an area of relational or sexual brokenness that needs to be addressed and healed in her life. It might be very uncomfortable and awkward for that individual to excuse herself from one group to go join the new recovery group that's being launched. The semester system delivers targeted discipleship, allowing people to pursue the opportunities they need at the time they need it. The members of the original group can still stay together, but the on-ramps and exit signs let people go in a different direction if they need to.

*More leaders.* When we moved to the semester system, we discovered that more people were willing to give small group leadership a shot. A finite commitment gives people a bit more courage to experiment. Who wants to commit to anything in perpetuity? Okay, if you're standing at the altar with someone, that's a moment to commit in perpetuity. But when we're talking about providing Doritos for the same group of people from now until the old folks' home, maybe we need to reconsider what we're asking people to do. An eight- to twelve-week commitment is something anybody can endure—no matter what weirdoes might come through the door.

*Rest.* Life happens, and every now and then, a leader needs to take a break. We can't take a break from our mandate to make disciples and live in community, but the Bible never tells us that once we start leading a small group we have to continue it forever for our disciple making to count. Life brings change, new seasons and mess, and leaders need opportunities to take breaks and catch their breath.

One of my very best leaders, Sarah Owen, had been leading a women's small group for way too long. For a couple of years, I had encouraged her to take a break. But she never felt the time was right to do that. Guess who took a semester off right off the bat when we moved to the new system? It was as though the semester system itself created a social construct that offered Sarah permission to take the break. It was for a definite period—like an on-ramp and off-ramp for leaders.

When we see leaders showing the first signs of burnout, we can encourage them to take a semester off. They don't feel like they're "quitting" or walking away for good. They're just taking a short sabbatical. There are certainly seasons when we need to take a step back from leadership responsibilities, but we can't take a break from Jesus' command to make disciples. Before semesters, leaders kept leading until they burned out, quit and never came back into leadership again. Now they take short breaks when they need them and then come right back into leadership.

*Momentum.* One of the primary criticisms of the semester system that I hear from small group pastors and small group leaders is that it disrupts and short-circuits momentum. I would argue that the semester system actually fuels momentum. I

**Some leaders will continue their groups with the same people a second semester, but they want to close the group to new members. We've found that closed groups are like closed people: they eventually implode.**

*MAEGAN HAWLEY*

don't care how great you think your group is doing, it needs a break from time to time. And in terms of giving momentum to the small group movement corporately at NCC, the semesters give us three strategic opportunities each year to promote our groups. Before we had semesters, there was no natural rhythm for highlighting group life, and it was difficult to spread the word about new groups that were forming. Now we can rally the whole church around small groups three times a year.

*Promotion.* In the three weeks leading up to a semester launch, we pour tremendous time and resources into encouraging people to be a part of a small group community. Each semester, we design and print a small group directory. It has taken many shapes over the years. The very first version was called *Small Groups Illustrated*. It had the look and feel of *Sports Illustrated* and included lots of pictures of leaders and groups in action. The next year, we shifted to *National Community Geographic*. Designed to match the actual *National Geographic*, complete with its iconic gold border, that concept was abandoned after I wandered into the magazine section of the Barnes and Noble and wondered for a few seconds why they would have copies of our small group directory on their shelves.

Today it's simply called the *Groups Directory*. And it's a one-stop shop for connection at National Community Church. Every semester, we print a new copy that contains all our group listings and contact information.

I'm not sure how many people at NCC get connected to a group because of the print magazine. My guess is that the majority still gets connected through personal invitation. The purpose of the magazine isn't to communicate information so much as to communicate value—the level of importance we place on community life at NCC. There are easier ways to communicate information about our groups. A simple spreadsheet would suffice and would actually deliver the data in a more compact, easily accessible and comprehensive manner. Spreadsheets are a great way to communicate information. But they're a poor way to communicate value.

Our small group promotion also includes videos of small-group members sharing their stories and occasional messages about the importance of community, discipleship and friendship. We're even experimenting with a text campaign.

## The Fine Print

Every small group model or system comes with a hefty set of disclaimers. No matter which model or method you choose, there are some inherent problems. It's messy. Let me go ahead and answer the next obvious frequently asked question: how do you create community when it changes so rapidly? That's a good question. As I said earlier, community experts and practitioners will tell you that real community doesn't begin to develop in a small group until somewhere around week twelve, which is when most of our semesters are ending. And in all fairness to them, there's a lot of truth and wisdom in that.

But we have lots of different types of small groups that serve lots of different purposes. Some groups are designed to help people get connected with other people in the church, while others are focused on helping people systematically take the next step in their faith journey, like the core discipleship groups. Many of our groups stay together as a group from semester to semester. Aaron and Kristin Mercer lead the Inklings group, which has been together for about seven years. In other instances, people within groups connect and then move together from group to group.

There's definitely a drawback. And there's certainly a risk that an individual could float from group to group every semester and never land in true community or grow in a meaningful way. That's something we need to be aware of. But the benefits of the semester system seem to outweigh the risks for us right now.

The point of this section isn't to convince you to run your groups on a semester basis. I'm speaking primarily descriptively of what we do and why we do it. I wouldn't necessarily prescribe a semester system or a quarter system or any kind of system for churches across the board. The rhythm of DC is different from the rhythm of Seattle, which is different from the rhythm of New Orleans.

Small groups should occur in real life—the real, everyday, walking-around life that the people in your community experience. Find that rhythm and flow with it.

## Discovering Your Rhythm

Another scene I really love in *Dead Poets Society* is the walking exercise that Mr. Keating assigns his students. He takes the boys outside into the courtyard, picks three from the crowd and asks them to walk in a big circle. When they first start, each boy walks to his own beat with his unique gait, but eventually they fall in line and begin walking in military-like rhythm and conformity. There's a tendency for us to drift into conventionality. When walking turned into marching, Keating stopped them and encouraged them to find their own style.

We do the same thing in the small group world. We hear about a "best practice" or learn about a resource or tool that made a significant difference in one church, and then we try to implement it wholesale in our own environment. The problem is that every situation is unique and every culture is different. What works in one place won't necessarily work in another. You have to find your own rhythm.

Discovering your rhythm is part science and part art. Here are some questions that can help with the science part:

*What is the culture of your community?* Are you in a primarily urban, suburban or rural context? A few years ago, I got a phone call from a campus pastor in an especially large megachurch who had earned a reputation as a leader in the small group movement. He wanted to ask me questions about how to do small groups. This was confusing to me, because all the people who had taught me just about everything I knew about small groups were sitting in offices right down the hall from him. The problem was that they had served primarily in a suburban context, and he was launching a campus location in the middle of the city. He suspected, rightly, that small groups in the downtown of a big city were a different animal than small groups in the gated community, Stepford, or Edgefield (that wonderful little subdivision in West Mobile that was my first land of bicycle exploration).

*What rhythms seem to be inherent in your community?* Are you in a university town? Is the K-12 school calendar predominant? Is there a dominant force in the marketplace that dictates a rhythm? For instance, a mining or agricultural town might be dominated certain cycles. A tourist town might move to a different rhythm. In Washington, D.C., it's the university calendar and the congressional calendar. In the theater district in Manhattan, the theaters are usually dark on Monday nights, but the weekends are extremely busy. Most places would be the complete opposite.

When you think for just a moment on this question, you find that there are interesting group possibilities that don't fit into the standard group diet of most churches. Maybe some early-morning groups would work well in your context. Or, if your church has lots of college students, consider offering some late-night groups. Marketplace groups, lunch groups and after-church discussion groups move the community schedule closer to the everyday life schedule. If you have lots of soccer moms, can practice time become group time? Know the culture of your community and be creatively relevant.

*What is the culture of your church?* How many times in the past year has your staging changed? If you have a different "look" every time the pastor turns to a new part of the Bible to preach, you probably have a culture that's always moving. If the organ has been anchored in the same spot since 1942, you probably have a fairly steady and stable culture. Frequent changes in vision, programs, campaigns and new initiatives may benefit from multiple semesters a year. If the culture of your church doesn't change as rapidly, your rhythm might be longer.

*What are the demographics of the people in our congregation?* This includes a number of questions: What is their age? Marital status? Are they single? DINKS (double income, no kids)? Families? Rhythms of life look different in all of these stages. Are you in a place that's very transient or fairly stable? If you're transient, you may find a more rapid pace in your small group rhythm (like three trimesters a year). If you're relatively stable, your rhythm might be longer (lasting a year or two).

*How do you want your small groups to grow?* Again, here are some questions to assist with this. How will new people find out about groups? How will they join? How will you discover and prepare new leaders? Will groups multiply and, if so, how?

Make sure you follow a rhythm that facilitates growth in your small groups.

*What is the role of small groups in your church?* What purpose do groups serve in your context? Is it primarily about community or growth? Organization or mobilization? Most importantly, what is your lead pastor's vision for small groups? What role does he or she play in the larger vision of the church? And what will his or her role be?

Making sure small groups happen in real life doesn't mean just paying attention to rhythm. It also means paying attention to needs—and realizing that an airtight model might not meet all of them.

## Speakeasies and Black Markets

There's a small group meeting in a basement in northeast DC. The members love Jesus and they love one another. They're reading books together and digging out the spiritual themes that they find. They're walking with one another through life crises like job changes, miscarriages and divorce. It's a group where community is being cultivated and people are growing in their faith. But it's not an official group. For this group, the beverage of choice isn't Cherry Coke Zero but Cabernet Sauvignon, so it exists underground. It's the speakeasy of NCC—a part of the NCC black-market small group network.

As Christians, we agree to agree on major doctrines and agree to disagree on minor doctrines. Problems arise when we disagree on what constitutes a major doctrine and what constitutes a minor doctrine. At NCC, we would characterize the alcohol issue as a minor doctrine. To add to the complexity of church life, every church has to make hard calls on how to handle the gray areas—with grace or with law. The alcohol issue is one that we at NCC happen to navigate by law. I won't bore you with all the reasons why or give you the play-by-play of the decade of conversations we've had about it. I'll just give you one quick story: When Carter first came to NCC, he was just coming out of an alcohol recovery program, and the first temptation he faced happened at small group. I made a decision then and there that small groups could operate just fine without alcohol.

But I'm also aware of the fact that some great community happens around alcohol. Like the Protestant Reformation, for instance. But I digress.

Here's the deal. Every church has rogue small groups. Renegades. Reformers. We call those groups part of our black market. Some groups are black market for the right reasons while some are black market for the wrong reason. Either way, if you want to have a small group system that operates within the context of real life, you have to develop a certain level of tolerance for the black market. You may even want to embrace it.

Renegades. That's how you could characterize most of our black-market small groups at NCC. They're part of the black market because they're noncompliant. They don't want to be on the radar screen, follow the rules or open themselves to new people. They try to avoid the mess of community. I'm not a fan of these groups, because I feel there's much that they can learn by being on the grid.

The danger we fall into as small group pastors is throwing everyone who doesn't want to do groups the way we want them done into the renegade camp. But I would argue there's another kind of black-market group: the reformers.

Reformers. These are small groups on the black market because they're doing great things but for whatever reason we can't grant them full citizenship status. The alcohol groups would go on this list. The group that helps men walk through same-sex attraction and therefore requires a high level of stability. The group that just saw many of its members become leaders of other groups but wants to stay together for higher accountability. These groups are great, and I may recommend them on a case-by-case and in-person basis. But we can't list them because either (1) we can't put our stamp of approval on them because it somehow doesn't fit our strategy or (2) they need to be invite-only.

When his disciples were concerned that an imposter was claiming the name of Christ to cast out demons, Jesus responded, "Do not stop him. For no one who does a miracle in my name can in the next moment say anything bad about me, for whoever is not against us is for us" (Mk 9:39-40).

Paul took a cue from Jesus when he wrote to the church at Philippi about those who were preaching with wrong motives: "The important thing is that in every way, whether from false motives or true, Christ is preached. And because of this I rejoice" (Phil 1:18). If they're for Jesus, we're for them.

Jesus and Paul didn't waste time trying to corral and correct all the rogues. Maybe we shouldn't either.

## The Gang

I'm part of a black-market small group myself. We are black market because we don't advertise in our small group directory and because we're not open, at least for the moment, to the addition of new participants. Most of the groups I lead at NCC are formal, on the grid, open groups. But this black-market group serves a need in my life for deeper community with trusted friends who have known me for a long time. It's called The Gang, and its members are the people Ryan and I would count among our most trusted, loyal and fun friends in DC. Or maybe the best way to describe it is that they're the friends who've had to put up with us the longest. For the most part, we all met in a small group back in the 1998–1999 year or in a small group that spun off that group.

When I think about the people who have been most instrumental in challenging me, inspiring me and discipling me during my seasons of life and ministry in DC, these are the ones. Now it seems we're all running in a million different directions, having assumed new responsibilities and leadership roles in our careers and leading our own ministries and groups. So our lives don't connect nearly as often as I'd like, but they're still the people I trust with my life, my spiritual growth and my stuff.

On one hand, they don't give a rip that I carry the title "pastor." It's not important to them. On the other hand, it's extremely important to them. They're willing to challenge me and ask me the hard questions because they want to see me finish well. They let me take the pastor hat off and stand spiritually naked before them—stripped of responsibilities, titles and expectations—just me, stumbling forward in my faith, trying desperately but often failing to love Jesus and love people the way God created me to do that. They give me courage through that process—and the courage to pick up the pastor hat and put it back on again.

Every leader needs a gang. The problem is, we're often so busy that we lose connection with the very people we need to connect with the most. Ryan and I decided at the beginning of the year to launch a black-market small group for The Gang that would meet once a month. All of us are leaders of other groups or ministries; this gathering gives us the opportunity to spur one another on in our personal spiritual lives and in those ministries.

Who is in your gang? Make sure you aren't so busy facilitating community for everyone else that you fail to experience it for yourself.

## A Quick Disclaimer

I think it's worth keeping the pulse of the ratio of black-market groups to groups that are on the grid. I think the number of black-market groups—even those that are in the good, positive, reformer camp—should represent a minimum percentage of your total groups. Otherwise, there might be a problem with your strategy or the way you're communicating your vision. One of the soft measures I look for is how many renegade groups decide they want to come on the grid because they recognize the benefits of being an "official" group, such as coaching support, training opportunities and promotional energy.

Many of us simply need to create space and flexibility within our system to allow for the existence of black-market groups. It can be frustrating, and it requires a healthy level of humility, but we may simply need to acknowledge that people can find legitimate community and be discipled outside our structures.

Often I've found that some black-market small group leaders didn't know *how* to become a group on our grid, and once we invited them in and gave them clear steps for connection, they were happy to be a part of the team. Occasionally we intentionally recruit black-market small group leaders to step into the mainstream of group leadership. Through a combination of casting vision for the importance of a unifying vision for group life, affirming their leadership and recognizing the role we could see them playing at a larger level, we're often able to incorporate what they're doing into our systems.

The key is to pay attention to what's going on. Where are communities forming, where are disciples being made, and how can you celebrate that? How many open spaces are available for potential group members, and do more spaces need to be created? Finally, be aware of what keeps groups off the grid and what keeps them on the grid, maximizing the appealing components of your system while recognizing that some groups will exist outside.

## Not Every Group Looks the Same

Here's a scenario that will sound familiar to many of us. Your group has been meeting for about eight weeks. You're getting to know one another; people are starting to jump into the conversation and even feel a little comfortable disagreeing on some points. They're laughing together, and prayer requests are moving beyond matters that affect their great-aunt's neighbor. You're feeling great because it looks like this community thing might actually work.

Then someone pulls you aside and mentions that he feels the group experience is just "too surfacey," and everyone needs to take their masks off and move deeper. He feels uncomfortable because people are just not being "real." He mentions maybe next week would be a good time to break people into smaller groups and talk very bluntly about sin issues in their lives. That sounds kinda right to you. Real community is about sharing our deepest places, so you agree to give it some thought.

Later that week, you receive an e-mail from a group member who mentions she would really like to get the group together for activities. Who doesn't like a little BBQ, tubing down the river, a trip to the rock-climbing gym and a paintball day? Well, no one except for that one woman who would prefer to do a group outing at that paint-your-own-pottery place. You ask those two to work together to develop some social activities for the group.

At the next meeting, you begin a conversation about what

transparency and authenticity in the group looks like. You even enter into a place of vulnerability by sharing some frustrating issues you're wrestling through with your boss at work. You open up the floor, and someone begins to dump her life story of abuse, the resulting anger and how that affects her ability to have meaningful relationships today—and by the way, why won't the men at this church ask women on dates?

Meanwhile, the rest of the group wiggles awkwardly, flips through their books, checks their iPhones. No one else seems to want to share anything. So you just encourage the group to think through what kind of group they would like to cultivate and promise there will be another discussion soon. In the meantime, we're going to do some fun stuff together! And your social coordinators pass out the list of events for the next five months.

Upon seeing the impressive listing of adventures and outings, another person speaks up and asks why there are no service projects. If we're going to be together as a group, shouldn't we try to do something meaningful together? We are, after all, a Bible study, not a social club. After that discussion, you commission that person to come up with some service ideas for the group.

Thirty minutes later, you finally start the study for the night.

Next day, you find out that one of your favorite people in the group isn't too excited about the group anymore. The sharing of the deep, dark, secret stuff was just awkward, and the whole thing about hanging out together every weekend seemed like too much. She was just wanting to be a part of a weekly Bible study. Not forced best-friendship and assigned accountability with a bunch of people she just met.

Some people think you aren't transparent enough. Others think it's awkward and weird. Some think you need to hang out more outside of group. Others just want a weekly Bible study.

What is the goal?

I will be eternally grateful to Joseph Meyers for his book *Search to Belong*. It gives us helpful language and frameworks for understanding the way people relate to one another in four spaces:

- Public space
- Social space
- Personal space
- Intimate space

People feel connected to your church at all of these levels. Some people come into small groups looking for social space while others come looking for intimate space. We acknowledge that most people come into groups looking for social space; we encourage leaders to aim for taking their groups to personal space; and we hope individuals will look for intimate space opportunities with a select few inside the group. That's how the Hungry Mothers started. Some of the girls that provide accountability in my life were relationships formed in a small group, but the small group isn't the context in which that accountability occurs; that happens outside of group time.

I think it's also okay to have groups that linger in social space and groups that "go deeper."

Another tension we often face in small group is the community or discipleship tension. What's the primary purpose for groups in your scenario? Are they primarily an environment for fellowship or community to happen? Or primarily an environment for discipleship to happen? Is it about making friends or making disciples? Is it about sharing life together or sharing truth together?

Some have argued that the most effective groups are the ones that hit the bull's-eye at the center of the spectrum. It's about creating community that facilitates discipleship and finding the place where truth meets life. Some might say that the sweet spot is found where we bring the truth of God's Word to the questions of life's problems. It's the tension we find when we ask our groups to be both relational and transformational.

Does every group need to land at the same place on the spectrum? At NCC, we've grown comfortable with the idea that some groups are going to be more focused on doing life together, cultivating community and creating environments where people can make friends. Those groups will be primarily relationally driven. On the other hand, there are groups that exist primarily to deliver content, make disciples and create environments for growth. Those groups are primarily curriculum driven. While I still think the best groups land somewhere in the middle (groups that lean more toward academic studies find that their discussions are more lively and more enlightening after they've eaten together and shared about their week), I think it's okay and even healthy to offer a diet of groups that exist on different places on the spectrum.

If we want groups to happen within the natural flow of life, we must embrace the idea that not all groups will flow in the direction that we want and that not all groups will look alike.

What's your rhythm? What's important in your strategy and what's negotiable? In what ways does every group need to look alike and in what ways can they differ? In what ways *should* they differ?

Most of this book has been about how to appreciate messes, contain messes and create messes. This chapter is more on proactively mitigating the mess. Establishing a rhythm, becoming less territorial about group life and acknowledging that not every group will look the same will give you tools to make the mess more manageable.

# Systems Are Made
## to Be Destroyed

*The only thing constant is change.*

**DR. JEKYLL IN *JEKYLL AND HYDE: THE MUSICAL***

In *The Creation of the Media*, Paul Starr offers the tale of the loudspeaker and telephone: "After taking power in 1917, the new Soviet rulers could have invested in telephone networks, as other nations were doing at the time, but chose instead to emphasize another emerging communication technology—loudspeakers."[1]

The leaders of the Soviet Union failed to recognize that the catalysts for economic growth had shifted the way communication most commonly occurred. Communication had flown from the government to the masses, but the channels were shifting to communication from individual to individual. Loudspeakers enabled a message to be shouted to the masses, but the telephone was becoming the technology of choice.

Today communication technologies have developed even further. I've never once used a traditional telephone to communicate with the teenagers in my world, and I barely even use my cell phone for verbal communication. The new preferred methods of communication are texting, Twitter and Facebook.

There's a tendency for us to cling to the old systems we've grown accustomed to, systems we feel comfortable with, systems that have benefited us and systems we've had a hand in creating.

There are many technologies that served well for their time: Siege towers. The horse and carriage. The typewriter. Cassette tapes. But they have all been replaced. Have you ever heard the story about the time the U.S. Patent Office considered a moratorium on issuing new patents because they felt that anything that could possibly be useful or beneficial had already been invented? Whoever had that idea obviously served as the chairman of the deacon board at his church as well. (I jest. I don't dislike deacons. My dad was a deacon.)

Some of us are still using telephone technology. Some of us are still using loudspeaker technology. It's time to blow up the system.

Sometimes things blow up because of a fatal flaw in the system or because of an accident—like the time we turned off the oxygen to our fish. But every now and then, you have to blow something up to give it new life.

Community is not an option. Discipleship is commanded. Both are sacred. However, the structures, systems and processes that we employ to facilitate community and discipleship are not sacred, and they should be routinely reexamined, reenvisioned and reengineered. When we get stuck in one system for too long, the program begins to take precedence over the people.

NCC implemented Operation Kaboom in 2009–2010 to rethink the best systems and structures for group life. Kaboom should also happen on a personal level; we need to ensure that our routines don't become routine. That means we need to kaboom our own personal spiritual practices every now and then.

We've blown things up a few times around here. It goes along with our core values that "everything is an experiment" and "playing it safe is risky." One year, we decided to move toward a semester system and implement more of a free-market small-group philosophy. That was a good move. One summer, we decided to turn all our small groups into short-term missions teams to their neighborhoods. Every now and then, you have to change things up.

Two years ago, we had a span-of-care system to support our leaders. Every two weeks, I met with a group of leaders called zone leaders. I had drawn these folks from the best leaders I knew and asked them to help me oversee small group leaders and give vision to the small group ministry. As the number of small groups grew, these volunteer leaders became overburdened, so we added a new layer of leadership and called them team leaders.

Zone leaders cared for and supported team leaders.

Team leaders cared for and supported small group leaders.

Small-group leaders cared for and supported small group members.

In my mind, this system made sense. It was scalable, sustainable and easy to manage. And it seemed to capture the spirit of 2 Timothy 2:2. And this system had been my experience. I could make a hard case for this structure biblically and practically.

And yet for us, it failed. I mean, at first it worked great, but over time, it no longer met the needs of our leaders. We needed Operation Kaboom.

## Divine Demolition

God initiated a few Operation Kaboom-like blowups in the course of his story. Sometimes God brought a tragic end to a sinful situation. Other times he just shocked everyone by implementing a solution that no one saw coming. The most drastic and tragic do-over was the creation kaboom we read about in Genesis 11, when God decided to scrap the bulk of his creation and start over with Noah and his family.

When his children were enslaved in Egypt, God rained down terror in the form of boils, blood, frogs, lice and even death to undermine the Egyptian religious system. On Calvary, Jesus kaboomed the temple—or at least the holy of holies. He broke through old barriers that kept people at a distance from God. In the future, he will destroy the earth and re-create it, making new heavens and a new earth.

I'm certainly not suggesting that we presumptuously assume the position of God or advocate that we go around blowing things up with reckless and arrogant presumption. What I'm advocating is that there are seasons and circumstances in which we need to stop doing what we've been doing in order to find new life— whether that is new life found in more time with friends and family or opportunities for deeper intimacy with Christ.

One of the greatest dangers of leadership is that we're tempted to become utilitarian in our faith: we read the Bible to get a word for another, we pray because it's part of our expectations, or we live in community because we're going through the motions. Sometimes we just need to take a big step back to gain better perspective on life, our relationships with others and what God is asking and not asking of us. Ecclesiastes 3 recognizes this rhythm. There's a time to plant and a time to uproot; there's a time to tear down and a time to build, a time to scatter stones and a time to gather them, a time to tear and a time to mend.

Recreating your system isn't always an easy process. It requires the humility to acknowledge that you may not have all the best ideas, and it requires the honesty to recognize that what worked yesterday may not work today—or may never have worked at all. More than anything, it requires a commitment to get messy and the patience to let some others feel the mess in order to create something new.

This chapter is the reason I never wanted to write a book that gave any kind of insight into NCC's small groups. I knew that once the book hit the shelf, everything could be different at NCC (like that discipleship map—I can almost guarantee you we won't be using that map by the time you read this).

## Slow Burnout

Driving back from Nashville, Leslie and I reminisced about lots of great times and great laughs. We looked again for the truck-stop sign in northeast Tennessee that carried the disclaimer "No Oversized Loads" to make sure we got to enjoy one more giggle at that. We tried to capture a photo of the Hungry Mother State Park sign in southwest Virginia to send to the dear friends who had joined us there years before for a retreat weekend. We reveled in the past, reflected on the present and reimagined our futures. And that's when it happened.

"Heather, I'd just be really happy to not be a zone leader anymore."

This is a conversation that's likely all too familiar to many of us. Despite our best efforts to equip our leaders, pray for them, honor them and lead them, they hit a point of burnout and look for the exit sign. "I'm just going to take a break." For several years, I had tried to help our leaders manage their burnout by taking breaks. Realizing, however, that we can never take a break from Jesus' command to make disciples, I encouraged them to think in terms of sabbatical instead of break. Taking a break is what you do when you want to walk away from your calling for a season. A sabbatical is what you do when you want to position and posture yourself in a way for greater impact in your calling. We wanted our leaders to position and posture, not simply peter out.

This situation, however, was different. Leslie wasn't burned out; she was in the wrong spot. "I'd just be really happy to not be a zone leader anymore."

I knew she was right. It was right for her, for her leaders and for our NCC small group system, but it still knocked the wind out of me, because Leslie was one of the first people I asked to serve in that role. Not to mention the fact that she was one of my best friends.

Let me back up to give some context. Remember that whole chapter on "growing people grow people"? Now (meaning the moment I'm writing this, not necessarily the moment you're reading this), we have coordinators who provide accountability and structure to leaders, coaches who offer care and support to leaders, and trainers who deliver skill development to leaders. But in the old days, all of those jobs were carried out by a team of people we called zone leaders.

Basically zone leaders were high-capacity, successful, proven leaders who could lead other leaders. The very first zone leader team consisted of Leslie Adams, Nathan Gonzales, and Brian and Kim Hill. Those were the people that made small groups happen in the early days of National Community Church. Later we added Heather Gonzales, Sarah Owen, John Hasler and Juliet Main. When I think about small groups at NCC, those are the faces I see—and the opinions, ideas, criticism and encouragement I hear.

We were about to enter a new era. Leslie had just taken a big step back. To be honest, the era had commenced several months earlier, when Brian and Kim announced they wanted to focus on some different areas of leadership development where their natural skills could be better invested. Again, I knew that was the best thing for Brian and Kim and for the system, but it wasn't a change I really wanted to make. And I refused to admit to myself that it was time to make some significant changes.

The final blow happened over the culinary wonders of Taco Bell. Nathan and Heather wanted to take a break. Maybe I should have fed them better.

Kaboom.

The entire first generation of zone leaders had quit. The Zone is dead. Long live the . . . whatever was next.

I'm telling this story because I want to be honest about why we kaboomed. Everything in me wishes I could tell you it was the result of my strategic, self-assured, discerning and downright stellar leadership. Unfortunately, only the self-assured part was right. And not self-assured about the right things.

There were a number of indicators that perhaps our system needed some revision. We were still running small groups according to the same systems and structures we had implemented when we had a dozen groups, when I was on staff part-time and when we were still one church in one location. We had not altered our system in any way to account for the numerical growth of leaders we were serving or the geographical stretch of our multisite church. And despite the fact that we had a semester system and encouraged leaders to take occasional breaks, our zone leaders never got a break.

On top of that, zone leaders were expected to be superheroes. They were tasked with recruiting leaders, training leaders, caring for leaders, ensuring that NCC policies for small group leaders were adhered to, navigating problems in small groups, moving groups toward multiplication, casting vision to small-group leaders, helping Heather develop vision for NCC small groups . . . It could go on and on and on. And did I mention all these folks were volunteers?

While we encouraged small group leaders to lead out of their strengths, we forced zone leaders to be all things to all people. It was time for a change.

I sure wish I could tell you that I initiated change after I looking strategically into the future. I wish I had been a leader who had the courage to make the hard decisions and have the difficult conversations when I knew a leader needed to be focused in a different place. I wish I had led. But the truth is, I had known for at least two years that a drastic change needed to happen, and I ignored it. The truth is, I was lazy. Implementing change is far more difficult than maintaining the status quo.

The problem is that one day the status quo blows up on us. In my defense, I'm sometimes loyal to a fault. These were the people who had made NCC small groups what they were, and I selfishly didn't want to change their jobs or remove them from their jobs or create a new system. I liked them; I didn't want to lead with anybody else. Lesson number one: the people that got you where you are probably aren't the people who will get you to the next step. Laziness and loyalty can be a dangerous combination.

There are two ways to bring change to a system. The first is to make small, seemingly undetectable changes that make significant differences. They don't cost much, but the benefits are invaluable. It's like the old airplane trajectory metaphor: one degree of change in course can result in a multimileage difference in destination. Sometimes those are the kinds of changes you need.

Other times, you need complete demolition. We abandoned our zone/team leader structure for coaching and caring for leaders. Blew it up. Leveled it. Destroyed it. And we started exploring how we could recruit, train, coach and care for our leaders better. Sarah referred to it as Operation Kaboom. The name stuck. And now we talk about kabooming all kinds of stuff.

## Demolition Team

Whenever I embark on a new adventure, the first question I ask myself is, "Who should be on the team?" Who should be at the table to brainstorm, pray, consult, make decisions and implement whatever crazy experiments we want to try? We called it the transition team, but it was really an engineering and reconstruction team. It included fifteen people—some of them were old zone leaders, some of them were trusted and proven small group leaders, some of them were staff and at least one was a relatively new member of our admin team with a heart for discipleship.

There are three kinds of people that I look for. First, who can bring something to the process? Whether it's demolishing, reimagining or reconstructing, we need people with skill sets that can help us precisely and skillfully bring change. Who can contribute significantly? It could be their set of skills or gifts. Maybe they have a keen sense of discernment or spiritual maturity, or an energy level or a depth of conviction that can bring momentum to the process. Years of experience and investment could be beneficial. Which people bring something to the table that's necessary for blowing things up and rebuilding? In *The Tipping Point*, Malcolm Gladwell calls these the mavens.

Second, who can bring someone else into the process? You need the mavens to bring the skill, and you need connectors to bring in the people. The vast majority of people are skep-

tical of change. Most people resist change, even change that
will ultimately bring good. To rally the troops, you need
some influencers on the team. News flash: If you're in charge
or have a position with a business card with some cool-
sounding title on it, you're likely not the person who exerts
the most influence on the average small group leader. It's
likely going to be another small group leader. Get those
people on your team. When it comes time to sell the new
vision, they will be extremely important. Who are the influencers who will own the vision, cast the vision and bring
others on board? In Gladwell language, those are the connectors and the salespeople.

Third, who can learn something from the process? This is
the person we often forget or whose importance we drastically
underestimate. There's always someone who can't necessarily
contribute much in the way of skill or experience and doesn't

**Yeah, I was the one who
had nothing to bring to
the table.**

*MAEGAN HAWLEY*

have relational capital but still
needs to be on your team. Often
this is a young leader who stands
to benefit greatly from being a
part of the process. Blowing
things up is a discipleship opportunity as well. Don't miss it.
I'm often surprised that these people contribute more than I
would have dreamed—partially because stupidity and re-
lentless idealism run with the youth. They don't have to un-
learn old patterns of thinking, and they see things with new
and fresh eyes. In Zempel language, they are the minions that
make all the difference.

The good news is that all of those original zone leaders are
still in the game, but they're playing the positions they're
better skilled to be playing. A surprising turn of events is that
the new administrative assistant we added because it would

be a good discipleship experience for her is now a part of Team D, where she's leading the charge on developing our training environments.

## Values and Execution

When we came together to kaboom, we initially laid everything on the table—our understanding of discipleship, our purpose for having small groups, our model and how we recruited, trained and cared for leaders.

At some point, you begin to separate your values from your model. What are your values? And what is the skin that wraps around the values? If we aren't careful, we get those things reversed. Usually people aren't upset with a fundamental value in our system; rather, they're simply upset about the way that value is executed. For instance, almost every leader I knew wanted to make entry points into small groups easier, but they also weren't happy with the concept of the semester system when it was first introduced. Instead of focusing the conversation on why semesters were important, we tried to focus on the benefit of ease of entry into a small group—which was a value embraced by many of the leaders. When people get upset about something changing, it's usually not a change in a value but a change in the way that value is executed.

> I wasn't on Team D before Kaboom, but I was a small group leader who didn't know what a zone leader was. Our entire system changed because of Operation Kaboom, but the everyday group member would never have noticed. We put all our eggs in the "investing in our leaders" basket because if the leaders are healthy, then their groups will be healthy.
>
> *MAEGAN HAWLEY*

Operation Kaboom was good not only because it brought a

needed change to our system but also because it helped us identify our underlying values.

One value was believing that small groups should happen in real life and according to a rhythm. The semester system was simply the execution. Another value was embracing the larger NCC core value that "everything is an experiment." The free-market small group model was the execution. We also value the idea that growing people grow people. Zone leaders and team leaders and our training blog were just the skin we put on the value.

In a retreat setting, zone leaders, team leaders and others who I thought could help us transition put up big pieces of paper and proceeded to write down things that were working well, things that weren't working well and the biggest threats or potential hurdles as we moved forward. We quickly came to the conclusion that two things wouldn't be on the table: the semester system and the free-market model. It's healthy to reexamine everything you do occasionally, but it didn't take us long to realize that those things were not broken and worked well within our environment. They were consistently recognized as two of the best things about our small group ministry.

**I'm not convinced we really put semesters or our free market system on the table. We may have discussed it, but I don't think we did due diligence in exploring other options. These parts of our system work, and don't need to be changed right now. But if we ever do need to change them, it's likely to be an uphill battle, and we'll probably end up keeping them longer than we should.**

*WILL JOHNSTON*

We realized that what needed to change most was the way we cared for, coached and supported our leaders. We threw everything up in the air, from initial training in Leadership 101 to summits to coaching structures to communication to reporting mechanisms.

Then the smaller transition team of fifteen met at our house to begin to dream about the future. Our lead pastor shared vision. We listened to presentations on coaching best practices from the world of athletics, military, marketplace, discipleship and parenting. We placed some questions on the table and proceeded to divide and conquer. Everyone brought recommendations and ideas, and we slowly began to rethink how to best support our small group leaders.

## Connections, Coaching and Training

We landed on a three-track approach to supporting our leaders: connections, coaching and training.

*Connections.* Our Connections Team is the logistical and administrative nervous system for our small group ministry. They make groups happen across our various locations and are specifically responsible for leader recruitment, leader registration and group promotion. We have small group coordinators who serve as the "face for the place" for small groups at our various locations. At the beginning of the semester, they help launch small groups and promote group life at their locations. In the middle of the semester, they shift their focus a bit from promoting to recruiting group leaders for the next semester. Our Connections Team drives the logistics and administrative side of group life, so when leaders have questions about deadlines, timelines, registration, promoting their groups and getting people involved, they get answers from the Connections Team.

*Coaching.* Our Coaching Team serves a pastoral role in the lives of our leaders. A few years ago, I realized I was wasting the time of some of our best coaches by asking them to coach and care for people who didn't want to be coached and cared for. I also recognized that different leaders needed different levels and types of care in different seasons of leadership. So we drastically changed our approach to coaching. We moved from a mandatory huddle approach to largely voluntary one-on-one coaching opportunities, and we focused the coaching more on the leader than on the group.

While coaches still help leaders navigate various aspects of their groups, their primary role is to care for the hearts of the leaders. Again, if a leader is growing, the group will grow. So the primary role of the coach is to ensure that the leader is being discipled, growing in his or her faith and in a healthy place to lead. If a leader is trying to decide whether to lead a group next semester or not, the coach's only concern is what is best for the leader, not what's best for our program goals at NCC.

As I outlined in chapter four, a new leader is assigned to a coach who meets with her or him three times to talk through her or his faith journey, what it means to be a leader worth following and how to cultivate biblical community. At the end of that first semester, the leader can opt in or out of continued coaching. We recognize that some leaders are already getting the support they need outside of our structure, and we're okay with that. There's no need for them to be in regular meetings with one of our official coaches just to check a box if they are in transformational community with one of our campus pastors or another leader or a mentor. If they do opt into coaching, the regularity and focus of coaching meetings is decided between the coach and leader.

*Training.* Finally, our Training Team equips our leaders with the skills, tools and resources that they need to become more effective in their roles. While coaches focus primarily on the hearts of the leaders, the training team focuses on growing their leadership gifts. This team fuels the content and creative development of our live training events, such as Leadership Summit and Leadership Retreat. They develop our Leadership 101 curriculum and ongoing, online leadership training modules. This team also helps us think globally about churchwide discipleship initiatives, curriculum development, discipleship pathways and how to incorporate those principles into existing group life.

## Kaboom Your Life

While we're talking about blowing stuff up, let's bring it down to the personal level for just a moment. It's not just ministry structures and systems that need to be reexamined, reimagined and rebuilt; it's also the systems and structures of our personal spiritual lives. Most of us need to kaboom our own lives every now and then. In the discipleship world, we talk about practicing spiritual disciplines and endeavor to create healthy routines. But when the routines become routine, we have to change the routine. Someone defined insanity as "doing the same thing over and over again and expecting different results." It's been attributed to Albert Einstein, Mark Twain and Benjamin Franklin, so nobody really knows who said it, but it's true.

Over the past couple of years, I've kaboomed my life in a number of ways. Here are a few that might be helpful to you.

*Celebrate Sabbath.* For years, I've found it easier to trust God with my checkbook than with my calendar. I honestly have no problem giving God 10 percent of my income and trusting him to do more with the remaining 90 percent than I would be able to. But I have a hard time trusting God with time. Some of this is rooted in pride. Some of it's rooted in the fact that I love what I do so much that I forget who I do it for. Some of it's rooted in a wrong understanding of what God expects of me.

Two years ago, I found myself stretched out on a bed, fighting strep throat and pneumonia. When the doctor told me I would be out of commission for a couple of weeks, I scoffed. I was too good for that and didn't have time for that. I decided to stay home for two days. Those days were painfully slow and boring, and I couldn't wait to get back to work. By day three, I really wanted to go back but just didn't have the strength to do it. At some point on day four, I realized I had grown to love the state of life I was in—a state where nothing seemed urgent, nothing had to be done except rest. And I had a much keener sense of what was truly important. It's rare that I hear the inaudible but unmistakable voice of God, but stillness and silence have a strange way of opening our ears. God showed me that I could intentionally celebrate Sabbath, or sickness would eventually become my Sabbath.

Sabbath is all about what we *get* to do, not what we *have* to do. It's about living in the place of rest and responding to what's important more than to what's urgent. Sabbath has become one of my favorite days of the week. I love Tuesdays because they're filled with meetings and activity. I love Saturdays when I preach, because they're filled with furious study and desperate prayer. I love Mondays, because they're the day I live differently from every other day.

Every Sabbath looks different for me, but I have two primary guidelines: What fills my tank? (In other words, what places, people or activities leave me feeling full and reenergized?). And what stirs my affections for Christ? (In other words, what places, people or activities make me love Jesus more?)

I always try to be intentional in four ways with my Sabbath:

- Plan for it. Without a little intentionality, I tend to waste it.

- Play with it. It's a day set apart to do what you want to do, not what you have to do. You may need to experiment a bit to figure out what Sabbath looks like for you.

- Involve friends. For some, Sabbath is a time for solitude and reflection. For others, it involves lots of interaction with good friends.

- Give thanks. More than anything, it's an opportunity for gratitude.

It will be messy. E-mails will go unanswered, houses will go uncleaned, and errands will go un-run. Celebrating Sabbath will likely cause more work at first. The children of Israel had to gather twice as much manna on day six to rest on day seven. In the short run, you may think it's more trouble than it's worth. Over time, you won't trade it.

Philipp Melancthon, a friend of Martin Luther and one of the primary theologians of the Reformation, is one of my heroes of church history. One day he said to Martin Luther, "Today, you and I shall discuss the governance of the universe."

Luther responded, "No. Today, you and I shall go fishing and leave the governance of the universe to God."[2]

In the midst of reformation and peasant revolutions and papal bulls and excommunications and inquisitions and translating the Bible into German, Luther went fishing. I don't know if he realized he was writing church history or not, but he was willing to leave the story of God in the hands of God, and he took a day to celebrate the provision of God, the creation of God, the freedom of God and the salvation of God. We would do well to do the same.

*Read a new translation.* Another way to kaboom your spiritual disciplines is to read a new translation of Scripture. I love my ESV Thinline Bible. When I turn to the book of Matthew, I know which side of the page the Sermon on the Mount starts on. I have a vague idea of that place in Jeremiah where God talks about the idols being like dung pellets and can spot the "LOL!" written to the side pretty quickly. When I come to 1 Corinthians 13, Galatians 5 and Philippians 2, I can just skim because I already know what it says. I can locate key passages quickly because the language and the layout have become very familiar to me.

The problem is that sometimes the Scriptures can become too familiar in a bad way. Sometimes we need to read a different translation to mix things up. We need to see a certain idea with a new set of words wrapped around it to give us a different perspective. If you typically read the NIV, pick up the ESV. If you tend toward the NASB, give *The Message* a whirl.

*Create a stop-doing list.* Hovering over burritos, they found consensus: "The next time we see you, we want you to bring us a list of three things that you're giving up. You've got to stop doing so much, or you won't make it." The Hungry Mothers were right. The pace I was keeping wasn't sustainable over the long haul. It was okay for a season, but the season had turned into months and was threatening to turn into eternity. We're inundated with encouragement to create lists of goals and tasks. But sometimes the best personal kabooms start with a stop-doing list.

The problem came when I tried to identify some stuff to offload. I couldn't think of a single thing that I could possibly give up. As I poured over a list of my daily, weekly and monthly activities, everything seemed to fall into one of two categories: something I enjoyed doing or something that someone else expected me to do as part of my job.

Cutting things out is never easy. If you didn't feel like you should be doing it, you probably wouldn't be doing it. I made three painful decisions that I was sure I would regret making. After I cut them out, my life simplified a bit, and I felt like I had some margin and could actually breathe. A few months later, it became obvious that I really didn't need to be doing those things anyway. My "no" became a much-desired "yes" for some other people as they were given opportunities that I had once hoarded.

Blow some things up in your life. It may get messy before it gets better, but if you want to grow, something likely needs to change.

## Kaboom Your Group

There's also a time for kabooming your group. If you're a small-group leader, you don't have to wait for some global change delivered down from your small group pastor. There are small changes you can make within your existing structures that are faithful to your current mission but still bring some change to your group.

If you've been studying about prayer for a while, maybe it's time to stop studying it and start doing it. That goes for a number of topics: service, evangelism, worship . . . Instead of having a Bible-study group, why not have a Bible-doing group?

One of our couples' small groups kaboomed recently when they realized that everyone in the group could benefit from focusing on financial stewardship. They ventured outside the box and handed over the leadership reins of their group to one of our certified Crown Financial leaders for the semester.

There are lots of ways to kaboom your group. We mentioned a few of them in chapter two when we talked about the benefits of experiments. If prayer has become little more than an afterthought or add-on to your group experience, move it to the beginning of your group time. Expand the snacks to include dinner. Or instead of eating together, use that time to prepare a meal for some neighbors or a new family at the church.

## Before You Light the Fuse

Even though I've written a whole chapter here, I'm no expert in demolition. I've never wielded a wrecking ball, operated a bulldozer or imploded a building. When I look at the moments when I have blown things up, I'm pretty sure that I did more things wrong than I did right. Here are a few things I would suggest as you blow things up. Pay attention to these, especially if you're kabooming a whole system.

- Be humble, be prayerful, be discerning. Don't blow things up just because you're bored. Make sure that God has initiated the process, and invite him to be a part of it all the way through. Humility is going to be extremely critical. To get the best feedback, you need to keep a thick skin and a soft heart.

- Be willing to hurt some feelings and offend some people. I remember when one of my zone leaders mentioned that I had "fired" all of them. I guess I did. I think he was just joking, but the reality is that you may offend some people when you change things. Some may get their feelings hurt. Jesus was a master at offending the right people for the right reasons.

- Stop doing things that are really good to make way for things that are better. Just because you've "always done it that way" doesn't mean you should keep doing it that way. This may be the hardest part of kaboom. There may be some systems or events that you really love, that carry sentimental value for many people and that even accomplish good things. But they're no longer the right thing. Be willing to kill good things to make way for better things.

- Try something that has never been tried before. Don't let that "we've never done it that way" excuse stop you from doing anything. If you want the same results, keep doing what's always been done. If you want to see something new, try something new. And I don't mean just trying something that you heard another church was doing. Cross-pollinate with the arts, business, science and technology to find new ideas. Our media pastor, Jeremy Sexton, once came up with a brilliant idea for a baptism video from watching WWF. Seriously. It's one of the best baptism videos we've ever produced.

- Meet with lots of people and cast lots of vision. Most people don't like change, but they like it better if they feel like they've had a voice, contributed to the process and helped to shape it. The more people you can talk to before, during and after the process, the better. My teammate Will Johnston is a master of this. Anytime he launches a new initiative, his calendar fills up with coffees, breakfasts, dinners and late-night hangouts with leaders who need to hear the vision firsthand.

- Be willing to see things get worse before they get better. Things will probably get really messy. We went almost a year with little to no initial training for new small group leaders, which created some messes. During our first year of implementing the new system, we had no framework for knowing what our needs would be, so the budgeting process was a crapshoot.

- Create a timeline and strategy. Ben Arment says, "Every idea is a spreadsheet with skin on it."[3] He's referring primarily to the monetizing of dreams and the importance of developing a solid fiscal model for a business, non-profit organization or retail store. But I think it relates to our plans for kabooming and reconstruction as well. Do you blow things up and then rebuild the airplane in the air? Do you rebuild and then blow up the old system when it's ready? How long will the transition be? Think in terms of steps, milestones, targets and strategy.

- Read the book *Switch*. Chip and Dan Heath have written a masterpiece here. This book gave our team new language, concepts and pictures for driving change and navigating the inherent challenges.

- Get the right people into the room. I've already written an entire section on this, but I can't emphasize it enough.

- Blow it up sooner rather than later. Operation Kaboom should have commenced at least eighteen months before it did—perhaps even sooner than that. I allowed loyalty and laziness to become my worst enemies. Many times, we wait until things get bad before we consider change. And by the time change is implemented, it's too late. In general, we have to blow things up when few people see that change is necessary. We need to change when groups are growing, leaders are thriving and the success curve is still climbing upward. If we wait for the curve to drop, it's too late. If we wait for the curve to plateau, it's still too late. Kaboom needs to happen when it will look like we're breaking a perfectly good system.

You're going to walk through mess one way or another. Either you'll experience the mess that comes from operating old, clunky systems that don't work anymore, or you'll experience the mess that comes from trying something new. Eventually either your system will break on its own or you will break it yourself. The goal is to break it before it breaks on you. It's easier to navigate mess that you create than mess that happens to you.

# Wear Out Your Welcome

*When we speak of hospitality, we're proposing something scary and radical.*

**LONNIE PRATT AND FATHER DANIEL HOLMAN
IN *RADICAL HOSPITALITY***

**W**e opened our door and walked right over our welcome mat just as we had done hundreds of times before, but on this particular day, Ryan noticed it. Our pathetic, shredded excuse for a welcome mat had faded. The word *Welcome* on the mat had been worn down by copious foot traffic over the past several years. We had worn out our welcome.

When Ryan and I bought our first home, we really wanted to make it an open-door environment. A place where small groups could congregate. A place where the church and community could cross paths on our front porch, where twenty-somethings could find a home away from home.

In that spirit, we chose our welcome mat carefully and discerningly. We selected one that boasted *Welcome* in a large, bold font emblazoned in the middle, surrounded by smaller translations of the word *welcome* in various languages.

On this particular day, we realized the big *Welcome* had faded, and most of the welcomes in other languages had disappeared. As usual, our perspectives on this mundane domestic development were almost as far apart as the loyalties of Red Sox fans and Yankees fans or the political views of Mary Matalin and James Carville.

My immediate reaction: that's terrible, we need a new one! Our house is a mess!

Ryan's immediate reaction: that's awesome, we're so hospitable! Our house is full of people!

It's not often that I like Ryan's perspective better, but in this instance, I'm willing to part with my opinion. It's true, we had worn out our welcome. And I think that's awesome. Here's what I'm learning: discipleship and hospitality are closely connected. I used to think that hospitality was about teacups and doilies. While those social niceties may represent a dimension of hospitality, at its biblical core, hospitality is primarily about inviting people into safe places to encounter the dangerous message of the gospel. It's about creating environments where people can experience the presence of God. Isn't that the most important thing we can do as disciple makers?

## Biblical Hospitality

When Paul outlined the requirements and qualifications for spiritual leadership, he never mentioned strategic thinking, vision casting, team building or communication skills. But he did mention hospitality. When I hear the word *hospitality* today, my Southern-fried brain runs to well-set tables and good manners. I recall with frustration the moments my wonderful mother tried to teach me the tradition of that well-set table, but I don't think these are the skills Paul had in mind.

In their book *Radical Hospitality*, authors Father Daniel Homan and Lonnie Pratt assert,

> Hospitality has two meanings for most people today. It either refers to hotels and cruise ships, or it's connected to entertaining friends and family in the warmth of candlelight with gleaming silver and ivory lace. One model makes it an industry, thereby assigning some productive use to it and making it profitable. The other model relegates it to the domain of entertainment and housekeeping, generally considered women's work. Thus, it has become safe and cozy, even productive, rather than revolutionary, risky, and world-rattling.[1]

The tales of hospitality that we find in Scripture seem to resemble this idea. They are stories of uncertainty, risk and sacrifice.

Abraham and Sarah were visited by three strangers. They fed the strangers and gave them a place to rest. As it turned out, those three visitors happened to be the Trinity. The return on their hospitable investment was a reiteration of the promise that Abraham would be the father of many nations. One year later, Isaac was born. (See Gen 18:1-15 for this story.)

The Israelites were spying in the Promised Land and considering their course of attack when they met a brothel owner on the wall named Rahab. She was scared to death. As she said, "all who live in this country are melting in fear." Spies behind enemy lines, treason and brothels figure prominently in this story (Josh 2:1-21), but the spies trusted a prostitute, and the prostitute faced her own fears and provided a safe place for them. The return on her investment was a nameplate in the genealogy of Christ (Mt 1:5).

Elijah was running for his life when the widow of Zarephath gave him sanctuary and first dibs on her pantry. Unfortunately, her pantry contained nothing more than flour and oil—and only enough for about one more pita. But as long as she provided for Elijah, her flour and oil miraculously reproduced itself. Fast-forward a few years: the woman's son died. Elijah's persistent prayer restored him to life. Hunger, need, a criminal on the run and death mark this story (1 Kings 17:8-24), but the courage and generosity shown by the foreigner of Zarephath reminds us that hospitality often triggers a circular domino effect that brings exponential blessing to all involved.

A Shunammite woman and her husband built a room for the prophet Elisha. One year later, the woman received the child she so desperately desired. When the boy was older, he died, but Elisha's prayer raised him back to life. (See 2 Kings 4:9-37.)

Perhaps the most famous teaching on hospitality is found in Jesus' teaching on the good Samaritan (Lk 10:30-37). The Samaritan, hated by the Jews, cared for a man beaten nearly to death and invested his time and resources in his restoration. Jesus' simple instruction was, "Go and do the same" (Lk 10:37 NLT).

Saul swept across the land, murdering and terrorizing the Christ-following sect of Judaism. Until one day when Jesus knocked him off his feet on the road to Damascus. Though terrified, Ananias (whose name means "God is grace") and the believers in Damascus took Saul in. His sight was restored, his relationship with Christ was affirmed and ignited, and his ministry began. The Damascus believers helped him escape from Jewish leaders who were attempting to kill him. (See Acts 9:10-19.)

Let's engage in a little counterfactual history for a moment. Imagine what would have happened (or *not* happened) if Ananias had not extended hospitality to Saul. The gospel would have required an alternate route to the Gentiles. One-third of the New Testament either wouldn't exist or would be written by a different author. Augustine's views on original sin and Luther's theology of justification and Calvin's understanding of sovereignty may have never been sparked.

Hospitality is ultimately about saving lives. It's about creating safe places and sacred places in the midst of uncertain and terrifying surroundings. It's literally about bringing salvation to people in need.

The book *Radical Hospitality* proclaims, "When we speak of hospitality, we're proposing something scary and radical. . . . Genuine hospitality is not cozy, and seldom makes you comfortable. It challenges, disturbs, unsettles, and leaves you feeling like someone is at the center of your existence on a major remodeling mission."[2] Practicing hospitality can take on a number of different forms.

## Refrigerator Rights

Several years ago, I led a small group that took the meaning of community to ridiculous extremes. They didn't seem to understand that small group happened only on one night of the week. Of course, my door was always open to them, but they really *had* to be there only once a week.

I remember one evening in particular when they called to ask me (or inform me, rather) that they would be coming over at seven to make pizza and to practice their routine for the upcoming NCC variety show. Fair enough. The only problem was that I had meetings at the church that would run well into the night, and Ryan would be locked in the basement doing homework. So I called Ryan, told him to let them in and told the group to have fun.

They came over, made pizza and turned on their highly creative theatrical skills to scheme up a MarioWorld skit for the upcoming annual variety show. By the time I got back home, the signs were clear that the small-group crew had been in our home. The dishes were clean and put away, and the kitchen was much tidier than Ryan or I ever left it. They felt like our house was their house. They felt at home, and they treated it like home.

If you work with people and with building community and haven't read the book *Refrigerator Rights*, you need to go get it right now. It's by Drs. Will Miller and Glenn Sparks at Purdue University, and it contains fascinating studies and perspective on the effect that mobility and technology have had on relational connection over the past several years. Consider the following:

- According to the 2000 census, over 16 percent of the population moved their residence during the census period.[3]

- One-third of young adults ages twenty to twenty-nine moved in one year—from 1999 to 2000.[4]

- Nearly forty-five million Americans move every year, and the average American moves every five to six years, thereby rupturing significant relationships with family and friends.[5]

These are some of the challenges mobility presents to our experience of community.

Also consider the effects of technology:

- Roughly one-fourth of America's dinners are eaten while watching television.[6]

- According to the Kaiser Foundation, during a typical year, the average child in the United States spends the equivalent of two months viewing television.[7]

We have barely begun to consider the impact of social media

on face-to-face connection. We have lots of anecdotal evidence pointing to both the positive and the negative impacts of Facebook, Twitter and other forms of social networking on feelings of isolation and detachment. I think it's a net positive, but if we're honest, we just don't know yet what the full impact will be.

In the midst of the messiness of community in a day of increasing mobility and advancing technology, Miller and Sparks offer a simple and profound test for community: refrigerator rights. Who has permission to walk into your kitchen, open your refrigerator and take stuff out without it being weird? I don't mean just opening the fridge to pull out a coke. I mean, who can take stuff out of your fridge and make a salad? Or cook a full dinner? The authors claim that the people in your life who have been granted refrigerator rights are those that you experience real community with.

Who has refrigerator rights in your life as a leader? Who has refrigerator rights in your small group? That's what hospitality is about—keeping your door open and your hand open for people to enter into your space. Hospitality is opening up your home so people can come in and do life with you as you're doing it.

I think the best hospitality happens in the form of the random gathering, where we simply open up our home so people can come in and do life with us as we're doing it. If we're watching a movie, come watch with us. If we're cooking dinner, come cook with us. And eat. If you need to meet with me but I have only two hours to pack before my flight leaves, come over and talk with me as I pack.

Ryan and I have always envisioned our house becoming a sort of ministry equivalent to Gertrude Stein's salon. A space brimming with networking, breeding creativity and challenging mindsets. A place to comfort the afflicted and afflict the comfortable. We've opened our house to gatherings of artists, amateur theologians and karaoke superstars. We love random gathering.

One of my favorite moments occurred just a few months ago. We walked into our house to find Jayne (my best friend from Mobile), Bernita (my new friend from Seattle), Andy (my NCC teammate) and three midshipmen from the Naval Academy sitting around our kitchen table playing Balderdash. None of them knew each other very well, and some of them had never met. But there they were in the Zempel house, talking, laughing, eating and playing like old friends.

It doesn't sound sacred, but good stewardship led us to purchase a karaoke machine, a large-screen television and Settlers of Catan, and those have proven to be excellent investments. Our next big decision is whether or not to invest in a soda fountain. When people come to our house, they know we're not going to set a table for them, prepare something special for them or cater to their wishes. If they're lucky, we'll ask them what they want to drink. The rules are simple: here is the fridge, here is the pantry. If it's in a Tupperware container without a clear date inscribed, beware. Otherwise, help yourself. You know where the movies, the games and the karaoke CDs are. Go for it.

Hospitality is going to look different for you, but the principle is the same. What part of your life can you open up to include someone else?

**We also have the right to clean Heather's refrigerator, and—let's be honest—it is more involved than helping yourself to a sandwich. (Maybe Will Johnston and I will one day coauthor a book called *Clean Community*.)**

*MAEGAN HAWLEY*

## The Table of Emmaus

The Road to Emmaus is a familiar story to many of us, especially those who grew up with the Vacation Bible School stories of the postresurrection celebrations. I'm on a mission to change the popular reference to the story to the *Table* of Emmaus, because the road wasn't the most significant setting. The epicenter of the story happened at the table.

Two friends were walking along the road to Emmaus—or perhaps it was a husband and wife; we really don't know. As they walked, they encountered a man who seemed to be ignorant of the news from Jerusalem: a young Jewish rabbi from Nazareth, who was thought by some to be the Messiah, had been crucified by the Roman government. Now rumors were spreading that his body had disappeared from the tomb and that some of his followers had claimed to see him alive. From our perspective as the reader, the whole situation is amusing because the author lets us in on the secret that the man they are talking to is Jesus himself.

Jesus then gave them a lecture on Old Testament history, the words of the prophets as they foretold the Messiah and scriptural interpretation of the things that concerned him. Can you imagine anything more amazing? To listen to Jesus himself talk about how the Old Testament foreshadowed and revealed him? To hear from Christ himself how he was the fulfillment of those words of hope and peace uttered hundreds of years before?

Even after a reasoned sermon from Christ himself on who he was, they still didn't recognize him, because Jesus didn't reveal himself to them.

Later that night, they sat around a table in Emmaus to eat dinner. In a scene somewhat reminiscent of the Last Supper, Jesus took the bread, blessed it, broke it and gave it to them. In that moment, their eyes sprung open and they recognized who he was.

On the road, they received reason. At the table, they got revelation. On the road, they heard a lecture. At the table, they saw life.

It absolutely amazes me that what opened their eyes to Jesus wasn't walking down a road with him or listening to a sermon from him. It was sitting at a table with him.

From Scripture, it certainly appears that more people see God's work while they're sitting around a table than they do when they're sitting side by side in a religious service. The most important family and religious ritual of the Old Testament—the Passover—was set around a table. The last night of Jesus' life was spent observing that celebration in the Upper Room.

The most significant ritual of the Christian faith—the Eucharist—occurs at the table. The early church celebrated Communion within the context of a larger shared meal called the "love feast." Communion wasn't an add-on to the service. It didn't feel like going through a drive-through and picking up an order of a stale wafer and plastic shot glass of grape juice. It was a feast. A celebration. The "love feast" is clearly referenced in Jude 1:12, and it's implied in 2 Peter 2:13, 1 Corinthians 11:17-34 and Acts 6:1-3. The purpose of the meal was to remember Jesus' sacrifice, encourage his followers and experience God's love. Maybe that's why most of us get more revelation sitting around a table than we do sitting side by side, facing one direction, listening to one person talk.

Ryan and I often refer to our house as "Emmaus House" because we want it to be a place where people encounter Christ, whether they recognize him in the moment or not. Inviting people over for dinner is where hospitality gets more traditional and potentially more formal. For Ryan and me, though, it remains fairly casual and low-key. Ryan likes to cook, so sometimes the dinner party includes a full day of preparation in the kitchen. Other times, we've entertained folks with the popular "cereal bar." (Purchase a bunch of those individual-serving, high-sugar kids cereals and several kinds of milk. Watch people relive their childhood . . . or live the childhood they wish they had.) We even order in sometimes. What we eat isn't nearly as important as the activity of eating itself.

## Fishers of Men

Some of the funniest stories I've ever heard or experienced come from my friendship with Jayne Fisher and her family since childhood. The Fishers lived way out in West Mobile, so far down Cottage Hill Road that no one ever went out that far except to visit the Fisher family.

Her father, Herb, had a habit of inviting people over for dinner but failing to tell his wife, Pam. On one particular Friday night, the Fishers loaded the whole family into the car to go into the city for dinner. As they approached the first stoplight on Cottage Hill Road, they encountered another car going in the opposite direction, occupied by another family from the church. They waved at one another across the intersection and continued on their way. About a minute down the road, Pam wondered out loud what that family was doing out that far on Cottage Hill Road. That's the moment Herb remembered that they were heading to the Fisher house for dinner.

I always loved the Fisher family for their hospitality. I've never been to their house without being served a Rice Krispies treat. They always had a random assortment of people living with them: missionaries, itinerate pastors from Japan, middle-school boys playing in the Little League World Series and so on. It was always fun to go over there, because you never knew what new experience you were going to have or what new people you were going to meet. I often found myself a little jealous of the Fisher girls because they were always making new friends with really cool people. I found myself especially jealous when those Little League boys were there.

Even now, when I go to the Fisher house, I fully expect a platter of Rice Krispies treats to be waiting for me on the kitchen counter. And I fully expect to laugh a lot, hear some great stories and have a conversation that shapes my views on faith, makes me hunger for God more or even changes the trajectory of my spiritual journey.

They've created a safe place to hear a dangerous message.

Inviting people into your living room and into your kitchen is one thing. Giving them a bedroom takes the risk to a whole new level. This is where hospitality gets more intense and crashes your world a little bit.

Ryan and I were inspired a few years ago while listening to Dave Gibbons talk about his approach to mentoring. When people ask him to mentor them, he tells them they have to come live with him. He recognizes that there's a dimension to mentoring and discipleship that goes well beyond the one-hour-per-week coffee meeting. It's about inviting people into the most intimate places of your life.

When we left that meeting, we immediately asked one another, "Who needs to come live with us?" It wasn't long before God brought those people to us, and I'm pretty sure the most significant mentoring and discipling flowed from guest to us. We've had family, friends, friends of friends, bands, social justice activists, missionaries, foreign service officers, sorority house moms and a gaggle of other interesting sorts stay with us.

Creating a place where people can stay with you may mean sacrificing an office for a guest bedroom or purchasing that clunky sofa bed instead of the sleek new model from CB2. Perhaps it means stocking up on some air mattresses and sleeping bags. But more than anything, it requires a paradigm shift from "my house is my fortress" to "my house is a safe place for people to hear—and see—a dangerous message." Hopefully what they see matches what they hear us preach—most of the time.

## The Front Porch

I'm learning that there's a critical connection between my platform—the places where my message is communicated—and my porch.

When I say "my porch," I'm not speaking metaphorically. I mean literally my front porch, which I never imagined I would have in DC. While I technically have an office space with ergonomic and helpful IKEA furniture inside the house, my favorite office is my front porch. It's the place I meet with God, the place I connect with friends, the place I coach leaders and the place where my world most often intersects with the world of my neighbors.

My porch is where neighborhood kids grab sidewalk chalk and help me map out a hopscotch board on the sidewalk. It's where the handyman working for Diane next door finds out I'm a pastor and proceeds to ask me a bunch of questions about faith, church and the book of Malachi. It's where my neighbor Wayne gives me grief for talking to my "Facebook friends" more than my face-to-face friends, like him. On my porch, my church friends and my neighborhood friends laugh together, drink together, discuss boxing together and challenge one another to games of cornhole.

My platform . . . well, that's more of a metaphor. The platform could be the stage I stand on when I talk to small-group leaders. It could be the trendy pulpit I occasionally stand behind at National Community Church. It could be the passions I'm known for. It could be my blog or this book. If I'm not faithful to my porch—that place where my message is shaped, where I encounter the people who shape my message— I should never have a platform. The character, relationships and dreams that are built and fueled on the porch eventually find expression on the platform, but I've got to live it first. Likewise, anything I say on the platform must be lived out on the porch. And the people who sit there with me know if my message is fueled by authenticity.

Don't aim for the platform; take time to sit on the porch. If you're on the platform, make sure you're preaching a message that you live on your porch during the other hours of your life.

You may not have a front porch, and for that, I pity you. But all of us have a place that represents the front door of our lives or a spot where worlds collide. Sure, it gets messy. Collisions are always messy, and they're especially messy when they involve people. It's stinky with that cloud of marijuana hovering over our entire block. It's a little unsettling when some of the neighborhood hoodlums yell obscenities at my innocent young friends from the 'burbs. But those are also the places where Jesus shows up, and for a moment we see heaven and everyday life smash into one another.

Refrigerator rights are one indicator of community. The collision of small group and neighborhood is another. It's not just about you knowing your neighbors. How many of your friends know your neighbors? How many of your neighbors know the crazy people in your small group? I love the fact that Wayne is BFF with Jenilee and wants to talk boxing with Jayne—even if it has to happen through the marijuana cloud filling the porch of the house between us.

## The Empty Nest

Ryan and I don't have children. But we've experienced empty-nest syndrome at least a few times. One summer we had a revolving door of the most eclectic people imaginable: A fifteen-year-old brother-in-law from Oregon who loves for us to expose him to experiences that will change his life—in exchange for some really great spaghetti. A student working on her Ph.D. in theology who was willing to talk at great lengths about trends in culture and how they affect our experience of church. A long-time family friend from Mobile who is now an engineer in North Carolina and is always up for a run to the Outback. An aerospace engineer and medical internist who are former NCC leaders and now invest their free time doing medical missions in South America—plus their two awesome kids. A couple of abolitionists who were heading to South Asia to put an end to modern-day slavery. Not only did their lives intertwine with ours, their lives sometimes intertwined with, encouraged and challenged one another.

When the summer ended, our house returned to a state of equilibrium and remained clean for much longer. Some of the mess dissipated. No more broken bowls. The toilet paper lasted longer. We controlled the television remote again. And it was very, very quiet. We reveled in the quiet for about 6.2 days, and then we felt the emptiness.

We learned an unexpected lesson: the blessings of God follow a boomerang trajectory. You just can't outgive God. Try to bless someone, and watch God bless you in return. Let's think back to some of the stories we addressed earlier: Abram and Sarai fed the three men and received a promise of a son; the Shunammite woman and the widow of Zarephath opened their homes to prophets who later healed their sons; Rahab found her way into the lineage of Christ. When we open up our lives,

God opens up his blessings and pours them on us.

Many of our guests overlap one another, which enables me to do one of my favorite things—facilitate and engineer new friendships. It's been such a great opportunity to learn and to live in community, and I'm thankful to get a front-row seat for watching God work in and through these amazing people.

In this chapter, we've moved from talking about small group models, methods and metrics to invading personal life. We haven't changed topics; we've simply turned the kaleidoscope. If we don't embrace the messiness of the organic community around us and practice hospitality, all our small group experience will stay in a safe, tame, sterile environment.

If you're a small group leader, disciple maker, mentor, pastor or whatever, here's my challenge to you today: invite people into your life by inviting them into your house. For dinner. Dessert. Games. Movies. Karaoke. A two-week respite. Don't just invite them in when the house is prepared for guests. Invite them in when it bears the marks of life. Bring them into a safe place to hear a dangerous message. Wear out your welcome.

# Navigating the Mess

I've been talking for a while now on the thesis that community is messy, but I'm still shocked every time it happens.

There will be messes that we need to clean up, which is why it's important for us to lead ourselves well and become leaders worth following. When we come to those messes that have to be addressed, we need to have the character, integrity and intimacy with Christ that will sustain us through that process.

There are times when we need to be navigators of mess. If growing people grow people, let's ensure that our discipleship programs are more relational than programmatic. Let's find ways to ensure that our small groups can flow to a rhythm that makes sense within the context of real life. We may find that we have to adjust our church calendars to accommodate our neighbors a little more, but that sounds like Jesus. We may have to grin and bear some rogues who don't want to follow our rules; it's messy, but we can live by Paul's idea that if they aren't against us, they're for us. It's not ultimately about us, anyway. It's about Jesus.

There are moments when we need to make messes proactively. Creating a system of nonlinear discipleship drives some of us crazy, but it's better to be effective and messy than easy to maintain and sterile. Blowing up your life or your group always generates some mess, but there's new growth on the other side. Inviting every group to become an experiment in discipleship inevitably leads to a few toxic fumes and hazardous spills, but we won't discover anything new and meaningful without them. When you open your door to wear out your welcome, you experience more broken dishes, dirty bathrooms and relational chaos, but someone might see Jesus in the midst of it. These are messes worth making.

## When We Make a Mess

Usually when I talk about messy community, I share examples from the vantage point of a third-party observer of a mess, of a consultant in the navigation of a mess or of a victim of a mess. But every now and then, I'm the instigator of a mess of the bad kind. What do you do when you—the leader—are the originator, creator and mastermind of an unintentional mess?

I found myself in that very situation recently. Short story: we included a humorous bit (well, we thought it was funny) in a leadership summit that offended some folks—including some folks on our staff team. The details of the scenario aren't important, but I thought I would share a bit on how I handled it. Or at least on how I wish I had handled it. Okay, let's just say these are some lessons I'm learning about how to lead and serve in the midst of a mess of my own creation.

*Affirm the relationships.* Relationships are more important than anything else—more important than vision, more important than strategies, more important than being right. If you have a small group leader or small group member with a complaint—no matter how valid you think it is or isn't—be sure to validate and affirm the relationship.

*Seek counsel.* I spent close to forty-eight hours doing little more than seeking counsel. As a high "thinker" on the Meyers-Briggs personality profile, I actively sought out feelers and others who could help me sort through the logic and the emotions surrounding the mess.

*Recognize your blind spots.* My partner in "crime," Will Johnston, summed up what both he and I felt at one point: "Enough people that I respect are offended that I am pretty sure I am wrong. I just don't know why." Listen to the people around you. It's quite possible you have a blind spot. Let me restate that for the record: you have a blind spot.

*Be honest. Be humble.* I felt it was important for me to be very honest with my reaction; I didn't just roll over and wave the white flag of surrender. I stood my ground on the decision I made that was in question. I honestly did not believe we had made a mistake, and I defended my team. But I also tried very hard to be humble and to say, "This is what I think; help me understand your perspective."

*Own it.* Somehow I was immune to the initial criticism. It was all leveraged against my teammates because they were the implementers and the ones on the platform. But the reality was that they were executing my vision. I had to own it. Even if I didn't have anything at all to do with the decisions and it was all my team's fault, I'm still the leader. I've got to own my own part in the mess.

*Keep a sense of humor.* I tried to acknowledge from the very beginning that "one day we will laugh about this," and we were laughing about it before the day was over. Not in a flippant or arrogant or dismissive way, but in a self-deprecating, "we're not going to take ourselves too seriously" way. We should take God seriously, not ourselves.

*Look for the growth goals and the leadership lessons.* One of my biggest goals throughout the process was to find the personal growth goals and the leadership lessons available. How can we communicate better? How can we better discern appropriate content? How can we anticipate reactions? How can we be more sensitive to differences of opinion? Whenever we're in the midst of a mess, ask, "How do we all grow from this?" and "How does God want to get glory from this?"

**The Summit Disaster of 2010 was a big upset. It took several weeks for feelings to dissipate, but walking through the process helped our team become more effective leaders. It was a real life moment where mess—even if we were the ones to create it—catalyzed growth. It has become a story—a story involving genuine sadness but also a story of grace, reconciliation and, I dare say, humor. In the end, we became a little more of a team because of it.**

*MAEGAN HAWLEY*

*Take care of your team.* My primary focus on the first few days of processing was to make sure my Team D was okay. Some of them are relatively new to leadership and to ministry, and I wanted to affirm them. I asked lots of questions that day about their feelings, their thoughts, their opinions and their ideas on next steps.

*Strive for good conversation, not final resolution.* At the end of the day, I'm not sure any of us found a perfect point of resolution. This may be one of those issues that we don't entirely agree on for a number of years. Maybe I need to mature a good bit before I see every dimension of my error, or perhaps this is just one of those moments when good people who love Jesus have to agree to disagree. What we must do is preserve an environment of open, honest communication and embrace the idea that the tension is good and resolution isn't necessarily the goal.

*Keep failing.* That might be the wrong way to say it, because failing should never be the goal. But experimenting, trying new things, pushing the envelope and innovating should be goals, and you can't do that without stepping into some messes every now and then. New discoveries are never made without failures. It's healthy for us to realize that we will continue to make messes. The goal is not to keep a clean lab but to ensure that any messes we make are cleaned appropriately and that progress is made as a result. If we're going to be leaders who make change happen, we can be confident that we'll make some colossal messes along the way.

I'm sure there's much more I could say. Stay tuned for the next mess of my own creation. I'm sure it's not too far in the future.

## Being the Body

Small groups are great. And then the people show up and muck it all up. Then our groups shift from sterile organizations to the body of Christ. A body that breaks and pours itself out for others. A body that carries the burdens of one another. A body that gets into the mess of each other's lives. A body where hope, healing and redemption are found. A body that bleeds, sweats and spits to seed a movement that brings change to a generation and a culture.

The difference between a meeting and a movement is mess. Let's make a movement.

# Appendix 1

# NCC Core Discipleship Groups

## Seeking Groups

- Spiritual Experiments: a safe environment for people to try out different spiritual disciplines in a casual, encouraging, no-pressure community of other experimenters.

- Holy Spirit Encounter: a study that focuses on the person of the Holy Spirit and his role in our lives.

- Sacred Roads Retreat: a weekend experience that introduces participants to five historical approaches to discipleship: relational, experiential, intellectual, personal and incarnational.

## Learning Groups

- The Story: a three-week, high-speed thrill ride through the story of the Bible. This group is typically offered in May Term. While our regular groups take a break during the months of January, May and August, we run a series of "May Term" groups that tend to be content focused and larger in size. They give people an introduction to community in a mid-size environment, and they also provide an opportunity for regular group leaders to take a break and be *in* a group.

- Old Testament Survey: a thirteen-week study that gives participants a bird's-eye view of the major people, places and events of the Old Testament.

- New Testament Survey: a thirteen-week study that gives participants a bird's-eye view of the major people, places and events of the New Testament.

- Bible Study Methods: a three-week, May Term class that offers participants practical methods and resources for studying and applying the Bible.

- Theology 101: a ten-week introduction to the core beliefs of Christianity.

## Influencing Groups

- Neighborhoods and Nations: a twelve-week group that introduces participants to the relational dimension of discipleship, including topics like hospitality, service, missions and evangelism.

- Leadership 101: a three-hour introduction to leadership and discipleship. Required for all new small group leaders at NCC. (We no longer offer this in a group environment. Instead it has become part of our online training.)

- Missions Adventure: because missions trips seem to be a catalyst for spiritual growth and the glue for community, we believe every NCCer should go on at least one trip during his or her time with us.

## Investing Groups

- Portfolio: a group to help participants discover their assets as Christ-followers and learn to leverage them for kingdom purposes.

- Crown Financial: principles of financial stewardship.

- Ministry: participation on a weekend ministry team.

# Appendix 2

# A Word to Smaller Churches

I love the local church, and I especially love the local small church. When I'm asked to name the most innovative and creative churches in America, I can't do it, because we don't know their names yet. I'm convinced that smaller churches are the best environments for experimenting with some of these principles, because resource and space constraints often ignite outside-the-box thinking. Small group ministry leaders and coordinators at small churches rank among my heroes, and they're the people I'm most excited to learn from.

Here are a few ways in which less is more for small group innovation:

- Planning for a leadership retreat for twenty-five leaders is a lot more manageable from a budget and administrative standpoint than planning one for 250. Not to mention the fact that you can make it much more personal. We had twenty at our first leadership retreat, and over the years we've built up to three hundred. The principle of the economy of scale has certainly worked in our favor in some areas, and we're able to produce a pretty impressive event. However, we've lost a lot of the personal touch, and it's getting incredibly expensive and unwieldy.

- Blowing up a system is less risky when you have ten groups than when you have a hundred groups. Having a smaller subset of leaders means you can bring them into all the conversations, prayers, decision making and vision casting that go along with a kaboom. If it's a failure, it's easier to turn the ship around when it's small.

- When I speak of things like teaching teams and discipleship teams and worship teams, you might feel discouraged if you're simply the discipleship person working with a worship person. Or maybe you're the teaching person, discipleship person and worship person all wrapped into one. Cross-pollinating between staff departments is much easier when there's a close relational connection and you work in close proximity. Larger churches have the tendency to fall prey to the silo effect—leaders working on their own. If you're small, take advantage of the ease with which you're able to collaborate.

- Churchwide discipleship efforts are easier to develop, unveil and promote when you have one congregation meeting at one location at one time. Now that we have to communicate new experiments and groups across several locations, important messages can get lost in translation, and I often wish I could go back to the day when I could make all the small-group announcements in all our services. Smaller churches have the ability to keep their messages and vision tight, clear and compelling.

- You can honor your small group leaders in more personal and meaningful ways when every leader is known personally by the small group ministry leaders and coordinators. Maybe publishing a magazine with listings of all groups is outside your creative resources or budget, but you can find more individualized ways to promote your leaders and honor them. For whatever it's worth, if you really want to publish a magazine, too, have a willing teenager in your congregation invest the time and talents to do it.

# Acknowledgments

This is my favorite part of the book. As I began to write this section, I realized that I didn't really want people to read the book; I just wanted potential readers to meet the people whose names are listed below and to be impacted by them the way that I have. Let me give you their names in the event you should ever bump into them.

To Ryan Zempel for putting up with more of my messes than anyone. I love you and love the adventure of our lives.

To Mom, Dad, Gran, Laura, Casey, Ruthie and Sarah for loving me through the whole mess of my life and for turning writing retreats into beach vacations. And to my Zempel family for bringing me into your lives.

To Mark Batterson for believing that an environmental engineer could be a discipleship pastor and for helping me find my voice.

To Margaret Feinberg for believing there was a book in me and dragging it out of me.

To the National Community Church staff team and leaders for letting me experiment and giving me grace when the experiments fail.

To Team D (past and present), the Hungry Mothers, the Gang and the Minions for letting me haul my mess into your lives and allowing me to display your mess publicly.

To Maegan Hawley for your theological sanity checks and the late nights double-checking my Scripture references. To Jenilee LeFors for motivating me with mean emails and milkshakes. To Emily Hendrickson for doing dumb stuff, laughing, proofreading and praying me across the finish line.

To Will Johnston for keeping me honest and for always cleaning up the Team D messes.

To Russ Robinson, Dave Buehring, Dave Treat, Mike Mathews, Herb Fisher and your families for instilling in me a love for community and discipleship, and for inviting me into your lives to experience it.

To John and Martha Reeves for giving me the perfect place to cross the finish line at Dauphin Island.

And to Dave Zimmerman, Andrew Bronson and my publishing family at InterVarsity Press for finding potential in my mess and for making it beautiful.

# Notes

### First Things First: Blood, Sweat and Spit

[1]DC Talk, *Jesus Freaks* (Tulsa, Okla.: Albury, 1999), p. 49.

### Chapter 1: Community Is Messy

[1]Mark Batterson, "It's Gonna Take a Miracle," August 17, 2009, www.mark batterson.com/uncategorized/its-gonna-take-a-miracle/.
[2]Francis A. Schaeffer, *The Mark of the Christian* (Downers Grove, Ill.: Inter-Varsity Press, 1970), p. 26.

### Chapter 3: Lead Yourself Well

[1]Andy Stanley and Stuart Hall, *The Seven Checkpoints for Youth Leaders* (West Monroe, La.: Howard, 2001), p. 11.
[2]Quoted in John Ortberg, *Everybody's Normal Till You Get to Know Them* (Grand Rapids: Zondervan, 2003), p. 169.
[3]Quoted in John Maxwell, *Becoming a Person of Influence* (Nashville: Thomas Nelson, 1997), p. 21.
[4]Henri J. M. Nouwen, *Bread for the Journey* (New York: HarperCollins, 2009), April 26.
[5]Quoted in John Maxwell, *Winning with People* (Nashville: Thomas Nelson, 2004), p. 84.

### Chapter 4: Growing People

[1]Will Johnston, e-mail correspondence, May 1, 2011.
[2]Quoted in LeRoy Eims, *The Lost Art of Disciple-Making* (Grand Rapids: Zondervan, 2009), p. 102.
[3]Rick Richardson, *Reimagining Evangelism* (Downers Grove, Ill.: InterVarsity Press, 2006), p. 15.

## Chapter 5: Discipleship Is Not Linear

[1]Stephen Sondheim and James Lapine, *Into the Woods* (New York: Theatre Communications Group, 1990), p. 99.

[2]Oswald Chambers, *My Utmost for His Highest* (Uhrichsville, Ohio: Barbour Books, 2000), p. 119.

## Chapter 7: Systems Are Made to Be Destroyed

[1]Paul Starr, *The Creation of the Media* (Cambridge, Mass.: BasicBooks, 2004), p. 9.

[2]Quoted in Mark Buchanan, *The Rest of God* (Nashville: Thomas Nelson, 2006), p. 220.

[3]Ben Arment, "Plan the Work, Work the Plan," April 5, 2011, www.benarment.com/history_in_the_making/2011/04/plan-the-work-work-the-plan.html.

## Chapter 8: Wear Out Your Welcome

[1]Lonnie Collins Pratt and Father Daniel Homan, *Radical Hospitality* (Brewster, Mass.: Paraclete, 2002), p. 10.

[2]Ibid., p. xxii.

[3]Will Miller and Glenn Sparks, *Refrigerator Rights* (South Barrington, Ill.: Willow Creek Association, 2008), p. 65.

[4]Ibid.

[5]Ibid., pp. 67-68.

[6]Ibid., p. 116.

[7]Ibid.

# PRAXIS
### EQUIPPING LEADERS FOR MINISTRY.

---

"...TO EQUIP HIS PEOPLE FOR WORKS OF SERVICE,
SO THAT THE BODY OF CHRIST MAY BE BUILT UP."

EPHESIANS 4:12

---

God has called us to ministry. But it's not enough to have a vision for ministry if you don't have the practical skills for it. Nor is it enough to do the work of ministry if what you do is headed in the wrong direction. We need both vision *and* expertise for effective ministry. We need *praxis*.

Praxis puts theory into practice. It brings cutting-edge ministry expertise from visionary practitioners. You'll find sound biblical and theological foundations for ministry in the real world, with concrete examples for effective action and pastoral ministry. Praxis books are more than the "how to" – they're also the "why to." And because *being* is every bit as important as *doing*, Praxis attends to the inner life of the leader as well as the outer work of ministry. Feed your soul, and feed your ministry.

If you are called to ministry, you know you can't do it on your own. Let Praxis provide the companions you need to equip God's people for life in the kingdom.

www.ivpress.com/praxis